MW00736467

Day Starters #1

Daily Devotions

By Dr. Louis Arnold

Arnold Publications
2440 Bethel Road
Nicholasville, KY 40356

Day Starters

© 2006 Dr. Louis Arnold
Published by Arnold Publications

First Printing, January, 2006
Second Printing, November, 2006
Third Revised Printing May 2011

Library of Congress Card Number: 2005910478
ISBN: 0-9727188-3-4

Printed in the United States of America

Arnold Publications
2440 Bethel Road
Nicholasville, KY 40356
Phone (859) 858-3538
Toll Free 1-800-854-8571

Table of Contents

FOREWORD

In the more than 85 years that I have traveled the King's highway I have learned many lessons. I have learned that God answers prayer. I have learned that He is near in times of trial, and that He is especially near in times of sorrow. And I have learned that God meets with us when we take time to worship Him.

More than 78 years of my Christian life have been spent in the ministry. In these years I have learned that my best efforts are not good enough to achieve great results. Only the power of the Holy Spirit can make our poor efforts bear fruit to the glory of God.

I have learned that God does not perform great miracles to meet small vexations. Great miracles are reserved for great emergencies. I have learned that much that is in the Bible is there to give us guidance in the dark days and through the deep valleys.

I have learned that it pays to lay up treasures in Heaven. The Bible tells us that when we sow bountifully we will reap bountifully.

I have learned that God speaks to us in different ways. He speaks to us through His Word. He speaks to us through providences, and He speaks to us in the still, small voice of His spirit. We must take time to listen if we want to hear from Him.

This book is designed to be a guide on the journey of life. There is a verse of Scripture, and devotional comment for every day in the year. It is my prayer that those who read these devotions will find guidance, inspiration, and comfort.

Devotions for January

January 1

A New Beginning

"This month shall be unto you the beginning of months: it shall be the first month of the year to you" (Ex. 12:2).

People have long observed the beginning of a new year, though not all nations have observed the same day. Almost 15 hundred years before the birth of Christ, Israel was told to recognize the start of the new year in the month Abib. That was in March or April, depending on the phases of the moon. Today the Jewish New Year starts between September 6 and October 5. In the Middle Ages most European nations observed March 25 as the start of the new year. We, of course, observe January first.

The beginning of a new year has long been a time to make new resolutions that are usually soon broken. It is far better to make new dedications to the Lord than New Year's resolutions.

The beginning of a new year is also time to take stock, to recount the victories and the failures of the past year. It is a good time to rejoice over past victories and to be thankful for past blessings. It is a time to reexamine and reevaluate past decisions, and it is a time to make plans for the future. Since we do not know the future, we should commit the future to the One who does. May this be a time of new beginnings and a time of higher dreams and ambitions for all who know the Lord.

January 2
Let Your Light Shine

"Let your light so shine before men, that they may see your good works, and glorify your Father which is in heaven" (Matt. 5:16).

Only light can drive away darkness. Jesus came to a dark world and proclaimed that He was the Light of the world (John 8:12). When we receive Him, we receive His light, and we, along with other Christians, become the light of the world (Matt. 5:14).

We are not to hide our light. In the verses following our text for today, Jesus tells us that we are to be like a city on a hill and like a burning candle on a candle holder. Our light is to be visible.

There are four things in our text that our Lord tells us to do. 1. We are to let our light shine. 2. We are to do good works. 3. We are to let others see our good works. 4. We are to glorify our heavenly Father.

We easily understand all of these but one. How are we to let our lights shine? As the light of the moon is the reflected light of the sun, our light is the reflected light of our Lord. The closer we live to Him the brighter our light will shine. In that light we can do good works that will bring glory to His name.

January 3
Be on the Lord's Side

"Then Moses stood in the gate of the camp, and

said, *Who is on the Lord's side? . . .*" (Ex. 32:26).

Spiritually speaking, there are but two sides, God's side and the devil's side. Everyone is on one side or the other. Those who have received Jesus as Saviour are on the Lord's side. Those who have rejected Him are on the devil's side.

To be on God's side, one must believe that He exists. One must believe that Jesus died to save sinners, and one must trust Him as their Saviour.

After receiving Jesus as Saviour, we must live for Him. It is possible to be a born-again Christian and still do the work of the devil. In Romans 6:16, Paul wrote to Christians, *"Know ye not, that to whom ye yield yourselves servants to obey, his servants ye are . . ."* It is not possible to serve God and the devil at the same time, so we should yield ourselves to God and work for Him each day.

It is a wonderful feeling to know that we are on the Lord's side and that one day we will be in His presence where we will shout His praise forever.

January 4

Future Glory

"We are confident, I say, and willing rather to be absent from the body, and to be present with the Lord" (2 Cor. 5:8).

God's people are on a journey. Unexpected trials are often encountered along the way. Multiplied thousands have comforted themselves in times of trial by thinking of the glory that awaits them at the end of the journey. The songwriter, Charles D. Tillman, put it well when he wrote, "And the toils of the road will seem nothing, when I get to the end of the way."

A missionary served in Africa for many years.

While there he buried his wife and children. When he was an old man he returned to America on board a ship. When the ship docked in New York he saw a great crowd on the shore and thought they had come to welcome him home. He was not allowed to disembark right away, and, while he waited he saw President Theodore Roosevelt, who had been in Africa hunting lions, get off the ship with his party while the crowd on shore shouted their welcome.

After the president and his party were gone, the old missionary got off the ship. There was no one to welcome him. Sadly he got a cab to a hotel and checked in. Soon he heard a commotion outside and went to the window to see what was happening. The president was going past in a ticker-tape parade. The old missionary felt very lonely and very discouraged. Just then the Lord seemed to say to him, "Son, don't be discouraged. You're not home yet."

January 5

God's Comforting Promises

". . . Be strong and of good courage, . . . for the LORD God, . . . will be with thee; he will not fail thee, nor forsake thee, until thou hast finished all the work . . ." (1 Chr. 28:20).

This promise, made to David, is one of many such promises in the Bible. Again and again God assures His people that He will be with them. We can make these promises our own.

The great preacher, Spurgeon, wrote: "If there were an ant at the door of your granary begging, it would not ruin you to give him a grain of your wheat. You are but a tiny insect begging at the door of God's all-sufficiency."

The following poem expresses well the greatness of the God of precious promises.

There's More

We only see a little of the ocean,
  A few miles from the rocky shore;
But, oh! out there beyond the horizon,
  There's more—there's more.
We only see a little of God's loving,
  A few rich treasures from His mighty store,
But, oh! out there beyond life's horizon,
  There's more—there's more.

—Author unknown

January 6

Jesus Cares

"Wherefore he is able also to save them to the uttermost that come unto God by him, seeing he ever liveth to make intercession for them" (Heb. 7:25).

Jesus told Peter that Satan wanted to sift him as wheat, but that He had prayed that his faith would not fail (Luke 22:31, 32). Jesus was concerned that Peter was going to be tempted, and He still cares when His children are tempted. It is good to know that Jesus is our High Priest, and that He can give us victory over all of Satan's temptations.

Satan is in the tempting business. He manufactures temptations of all kinds. He makes normal temptations that are sufficient to cause weak Christians to stumble. He makes stronger temptations to use on those who are not easily led astray. He even makes temptations that men have never had to bear.

Jesus is able to give victory over them all. When

Satan boxes us in, Jesus makes an opening so we can escape. When Satan tempts us beyond our endurance, Jesus gives added grace. If Satan tries to put one of his really big temptations on us, one that men have never had to endure, Jesus steps up and tells him that he cannot use that temptation. See 1 Cor. 10:13. Jesus understands our suffering, our sorrow, and our temptations. Claim His promises and bring Him your burdens and your temptations today. You can have the victory.

January 7

The Good Shepherd

"I am the good shepherd, and know my sheep . . ." (John 10:14).

Jesus lived in the world as a man, so He knows our needs and our trials. He knows what it is like to be ignored and neglected. *"He came unto his own, and His own received him not"* (John 1:11). He knows what it is like to suffer. He knows what it is like to be tempted. He was tempted at all points as we are, yet without sin.

We do not all have the same weaknesses, the same trials, or the same temptations, but no matter what we have to go through Jesus understands.

He understands homesickness. He was exiled far from home for more than thirty-three years. He understands our sorrow. He wept at the tomb of Lazarus. He understands our burden for the lost. He wept over a lost world. He knows what it is like to be tired, thirsty, and hungry. He knows what it is like to be forsaken.

He knows what it is like to suffer. He was scourged, crowned with thorns, and nailed to a cross.

He even knows what it is like to die.

No matter what our need, He understands and is ready to help us. He is only a prayer away. Bring your burdens to Him today.

January 8
God Speaks

"GOD, who at sundry times and in divers manners spake in time past unto the fathers by the prophets, Hath in these last days spoken unto us by his Son, whom he hath appointed heir of all things, by whom also he made the worlds" (Heb. 1:1, 2).

Ponder these marvelous verses. They speak of God the Father and God the Son. They speak of the creation of the worlds, of the prophets, and of the fact that God has spoken to man in various ways in the past. Most importantly, they tell us that God has spoken to us by His Son.

God spoke to people in times past, and He speaks to us today. He speaks to us through His Word, and He speaks to us through the Holy Spirit. God is interested in us, and He wants to lead us in paths of righteousness. We should be open to His leading at all times. When we do not know which way to turn, we should wait until the Lord makes the way plain to us. We should not run ahead of the Lord or lag behind when He makes His will clear to us. God's way is the way of victory and blessings. Find His way and continue in it.

January 9
The Sure Foundation

"For ever, O LORD, thy word is settled in heaven" (Psa. 119:89).

God's Word is settled in Heaven, and it is also settled on earth. *By the Word of God the worlds were formed* (Heb. 11:3). Jesus was the Word in the beginning (John 1:1, 2). Later, holy men of God, moved by the Holy Spirit, gave us God's Word in written form. That Word has been preserved through the ages, and today we have it in bound copies that we call the Bible. For centuries enemies of the Word of God have tried to discredit it, but all their efforts have failed. They will also fail in the future. The Word of God is settled in Heaven and it cannot be destroyed. Well has an unknown poet written:

The Blacksmith's Anvil

Last eve I paused beside a blacksmith's door
  And heard the anvils ring the vesper chime.
Then looking in, I saw upon the floor,
  Old hammers worn with beating years of time.
"How many anvils have you had?" asked I,
  "To wear and batter all those hammers so?"
"Just one," he said with twinkling eye.
  "The anvil wear the hammers out, you know."
And so, thought I, the anvil of God's Word
  For ages skeptic blows have beat upon.
Though the noise of falling blows was heard
  The anvil is unharmed—the hammers gone.

January 10

Reasons to Be Thankful

"Enter into his gates with thanksgiving, and into his courts with praise: . . ." (Psa. 100:4).

The 100th Psalm is a praise Psalm. It begins by telling us to make a joyful noise unto the Lord. It continues by telling us to serve Him with gladness and come into His presence with singing. There is nothing negative here. This psalm is all joy and gladness.

It is not easy to praise God when things go wrong. It is human to complain, and it is human to only rejoice when things go well. The children of Israel did not rejoice when Pharaoh's army was pursuing them and their way was blocked by the sea. They only rejoiced after Pharaoh's army was destroyed and they were safely across the sea. They could have rejoiced by faith before they crossed the sea, but they did not. They were walking by sight instead of walking by faith. It is a mark of spiritual maturity to rejoice and praise God before the victory comes.

January 11

Light for the Journey

"The entrance of thy words giveth light . . ." (Psa. 119:130).

"So then faith cometh by hearing, and hearing by the word of God" (Rom. 10:17).

Unsaved people walk in darkness, because Satan blinds their minds. Only the Word of God can bring them light and saving faith. After a person is saved, the Word of God gives them light for the journey.

A Christian man, packing for a journey, said to a friend: "There is a little corner in my suitcase where I will pack a guidebook, a lamp, a mirror, a telescope, a bundle of old letters, a book of poems, several biographies, a hymnbook, a sharp sword, a small library containing 66 books, and all these articles will fit into a space of about 6 by 9 inches."

"How is that possible?" the friend asked.

"Easily. The Bible contains all these things," he replied.

The Word of God does contain all that and more. Read it often and hide its teachings in your heart. Live by its precepts. It will give you light for the journey.

January 12

The Value of Trials

"That the trial of your faith, being much more precious than of gold that perisheth, . . ." (1 Pet. 1:7).

As heat refines gold and makes it beautiful, trials burn the dross out of our lives. Trials are not easy to endure, but there are lessons to be learned from them.

Trials teach us to rely upon God. Often we do not turn to God until there is nowhere else to turn.

Trials make us sympathetic. Only after we have suffered can we truly understand the suffering of others. Only one who has sorrowed can understand those who are walking through the valley of sorrow.

Trials can make us homesick for Heaven. If we never had sorrow, trouble, sickness, or disappointment, there would be no desire to go to Heaven. Only after we have experienced winter's cold, summer's heat, disappointment, failure, loneliness, sickness, and sorrow can we truly appreciate the better country God has prepared for those who love Him.

We must learn to cherish our trials, and praise God for them. They are more precious than gold.

January 13

Keeping Our First Love

"Nevertheless I have somewhat against thee, be-cause thou hast left thy first love" (Rev. 2:4).

Remember the love, and joy, and enthusiasm that filled your heart when you were first saved. It was as if your feet had wings. You felt that you could fly across any valley, climb any mountain, and conquer any obstacle that was in your way. After such an experience, all too often the glory begins to fade. When that happens, we need to come back to the Lord, spend time with Him, and renew our commitment to Him.

We need more than the ashes of yesterday's fire upon the altar of our hearts. We need more than the stale manna that was left over from yesterday's gatherings. We need more than the answers to yesterday's prayers. We need a fresh experience with the Lord so we can face today's problems and meet today's trials.

We need to return to the first love and do the first works. In that way we can enjoy the Lord's presence through the day, and we can end the day with the Lord's commendation, *"His lord said unto him, Well done, thou good and faithful servant"* (Mat. 25:21).

January 14

Growing in Grace

"But grow in grace, and in the knowledge of our Lord and Saviour Jesus Christ. . . ." (2 Pet. 3:18).

In some ways the Christian life is similar to the natural life. When a baby is born it must be fed and cared for. In time it grows, gains strength, and learns to walk. The process of growing continues until the baby reaches adulthood. Growing in knowledge can last for many years, even for most of one's life.

The Christian life also begins with a birth, and a newborn Christian needs care and feeding in order to grow in the Lord. Sadly, some Christians grow little and never reach maturity. When that happens it is usually because of the neglect of the proper growing conditions.

A newborn baby is not left outside in the cold to fend for itself. It must be clothed, loved, fed, and cared for. A baby would do as well outside on a cold winter day as a new Christian will do in a cold, sinful world. A new Christian belongs in a warm, loving, spiritual church.

We need to contribute to their own spiritual growth. They need to feed upon the Word of God. They need to pray and worship the Lord daily, and they need to be active in the Lord's service.

January 15

Avoiding Temptation

"Watch and pray, that ye enter not into temptation: the spirit indeed is willing, but the flesh is weak" (Matt. 26:41).

Temptation comes to all of us. It is not always easy to say no when temptation comes, but there are ways we can keep from yielding.

We can learn much from the temptation and fall of Eve (Gen. 3:1-6). She was alone and in a vulnerable position. She was near the object of temptation, and she was in the presence of Satan. She listened to Satan, believed his lie, looked at the forbidden fruit and desired it. It is little wonder that she partook of the forbidden fruit and led Adam to partake also. From Eve's experience we learn that we should not linger near the object of temptation. We should leave the object of temptation and resist Satan. We are promised that he will flee from us when we resist him (James 4:7).

To avoid temptation we should stay close to Jesus. Satan cannot stay in His presence. We should pray for strength to overcome temptation, and we should trust the Lord for victory.

January 16

Needed Vision

"And Elisha prayed, and said, LORD, I pray thee, open his eyes, that he may see. . . ." (2 Kings 6:17).

The king of Syria was making war against Israel. More than twice Elisha, who was living with his servant in Dothan, had told the king of Israel where the armies of Syria were located and how to avoid them. The king of Syria learned that Elijah was telling the king of Israel how to avoid him, and he sent a great host of men and chariots to Dothan to capture the prophet.

The next morning Elisha's servant saw the army surrounding Dothan and cried out in fear. He was afraid because he did not have faith to believe that God would save him and his master.

Elisha prayed for the Lord to open his servant's eyes so he could see the deliverance God had prepared for them. The servant's eyes were opened, and he saw the mountains around them filled with horses and chariots of fire. He saw that the forces that were for them were far more than the forces that were against them.

We also need our spiritual eyes opened. We need to understand that the One who is for us is greater than the one who is against us (1 John 4:4). Our God is able to answer our prayers, to vanquish our foes, and to give us victory against great odds.

January 17
The Value of Tears

". . . I have heard thy prayer, I have seen thy tears: . . ." (Isa. 38:5).

Tears are a gift from God. They were designed to drain the bitterness from a breaking heart. If it were possible to analyze a tear, we would find that it contained saline solution, fragments of a broken heart, and a mixture of blasted dreams.

As far as we know there were no tears before Adam and Eve sinned, but there have been tears ever since. Through the ages brokenhearted humans have shed enough tears to fill all the oceans of the world. There will be tears as long as we live in a sinful world. They will only end when we live in Heaven and God shall wipe them all away.

God takes note of our tears. When Isaiah told King Hezekiah that he was going to die, he turned his face to the wall and wept and prayed. Then God sent Isaiah to tell him that He had heard his prayer and seen his tears.

When we have cause for tears, God knows and cares. He still sees our tears and answers our prayers.

January 18
The Power of Influence

"And Israel served the LORD all the days of

Joshua, and all the days of the elders that overlived Joshua . . ." (Josh. 24:31).

Joshua had an influence while he lived, and his influence lived on after he was gone. So great was the impact of his life that he led a nation to serve the Lord, and his influence lived on in the lives of his associates after his death. Israel continued to serve the Lord as long as they lived.

When people live in sin, their children usually follow them in sin. God tells us in His Word that the iniquities of the fathers are visited upon their children to the third and fourth generation. Conversely, when people live for God, their children usually live for God.

The influence of a godly life makes for a happier home. A godly influence in the workplace is a blessing. Others are often influenced to be more productive and more loyal to supervisors. Also, such an influence often causes others to become Christians. We should all let our lights shine every day to the glory of God.

January 19

A Good Testimony

"For he was a good man, and full of the Holy Ghost and of faith: and much people was added unto the Lord" (Acts 11:24).

This was written of Barnabas, an associate of the Apostle Paul, during his early missionary work. Barnabas was a man to admire, and he set an example for us to follow. Every Christian should be a good person. Christians should have good dispositions. They should not speak in anger. They should be gentle, kind, cooperative, outgoing, and helpful. They should be Christlike, and they should bear the fruit of the Spirit.

Barnabas was filled with the Holy Spirit. We too should be filled with the Holy Spirit (Eph. 5:18). Only as we are filled and led by the Spirit can we be the kind of people God wants us to be.

Barnabas was full of faith. We all need the kind of faith that drives away doubt and fear. We should have faith to take our burdens to the Lord and leave them there. We should have faith to get answers to our prayers.

Barnabas was a soul winner. He set an example for us to follow. God grant that it can be said of us, as it was of Barnabas, *"and much people was added unto the Lord."*

January 20

The Way to Prosper

"Thus saith the LORD, thy Redeemer, the Holy One of Israel; I am the LORD thy God which teacheth thee to profit, which leadeth thee by the way that thou shouldest go" (Isa. 48:17).

God wants His people to prosper. In our text He has promised to teach us to prosper. In the first Psalm we are told that a godly man will prosper in all that he does. But we are not promised that we will prosper when we are out of the Lord's will. We must live in God's will and walk in God's way if we want God to teach us to prosper.

God knows what we can do best, and He knows where we can best serve Him. We are not to lean on our own understanding (Prov. 3:5). We are to let God lead us. When we are in the place of His leading and in the occupation of His choosing, He has promised that He will teach us how to prosper. Many who have failed time after time have found success when they learned to let God lead them.

A man who had failed in the dry cleaning business four times told me that he never prospered until he took God as his partner. After that he started prospering far beyond his expectations. Now he was meeting every customer with a smile, and constantly witnessing for God. He was one of many such examples I have met on the road of life.

If you want to prosper, turn your life over to God and trust Him to lead you and bless you.

January 21

Rejoice in God's Blessings

"The LORD bless thee, and keep thee: The LORD make his face shine upon thee, and be gracious unto thee: The LORD lift up his countenance upon thee, and give thee peace" (Num. 6:24-26).

Our text contains the blessing that the Lord gave Moses to pass on to Aaron and his sons. With these words they were to bless the children of Israel.

Great blessings are contained in these few words. They were promised that God would bless them, keep them, make His face shine upon them, be gracious unto them, lift up His countenance upon them, and give them peace.

Israel was God's chosen nation, and God gave the people of Israel special blessings. Christians are also chosen of God (1 Pet. 2:9), and we have a right to expect and to claim God's blessings as well. We are God's children, born into His family. We call God our Father, and He calls us His children. We are citizens of Heaven, and we are heirs and joint heirs with Jesus Christ. God loves us, and His blessings rest upon us. Let us rejoice in His blessings and in the privilege of serving Him.

January 22

Words of Confidence

"For the Lord GOD will help me; therefore shall I not be confounded (confused)*: therefore have I set my face like a flint, and I know that I shall not be ashamed* (embarrassed)*"* (Isa. 50:7).

The verse preceding our text is a prediction of the shame and suffering Jesus was to endure before He was nailed to the cross. Our text is an expression of the faith and confidence that would sustain Him in that hour.

As Jesus claimed these promises in His greatest hour of trial, we can claim them in the tiny trials we have to face. The Lord God will help us. We need not be confused; His Spirit will lead us. We must set our faces like a flint to do the will of God. In His will we need never be embarrassed.

We should claim the promises of God for our life today. There is so much that we do not know, so much that we do not understand, we need His help every day. That is one of many reasons why we should start every day with God. May God bless you and keep you in His will today.

January 23

The Way of Victory

"Looking unto Jesus the author and finisher of our faith, . . ." (Heb. 12:2).

Looking unto Jesus is not the same as looking at Him. The world looks at Him with curiosity. We look unto Him in faith. To many, He is only a man of history. To Christians, He is the Son of God, the Lord and Saviour, and their soon coming King.

Jesus is the author of our faith. One definition of author is "originator or creator." Jesus is the originator of our faith, and He will stay with us to the end. We cannot start the Christian race without Him, and we cannot finish it without Him. As the finisher of our faith, He will see us safely through to the end of our journey.

The chapter preceding our text is the great faith chapter of the Bible. It lists past heroes of faith then tells us in the last verse that they were not perfect, or complete without us. There have been heroes of faith in all ages, and there are heroes of faith today. The God who finished their faith will also finish our faith. Let us continue the journey *"looking unto Jesus."*

January 24

Manna from Heaven

"Our fathers did eat manna in the desert; . . . He gave them bread from heaven to eat. I am the living bread which came down from heaven, . . ." (John 6:31, 51).

During the forty years the children of Israel journeyed in the wilderness, God fed them manna from Heaven. That manna was a type of Jesus. He is the true bread from Heaven.

The people were to gather fresh manna every day except on the Sabbath. Each day they were to gather only enough for that day. If they tried to gather enough for two days and keep it overnight it spoiled. That tells us that we should gather fresh manna from Heaven every morning. What a beautiful type. If we do not come into the Father's presence for fresh blessings each day, our spiritual life will grow stale. Jesus is ready to give us bread from Heaven each day. He knows what we need, and He is ready to supply that need. After the disciples had fished all night and caught nothing, Jesus met them on the shore in the morning with bread and fish prepared for them. He knew that they were tired, discouraged, and hungry, and He met their need. Just so, He knows what we need, and He is ready and able to supply that need.

January 25

God's Imparted Love

"Beloved, let us love one another: for love is of God; and every one that loveth is born of God, and knoweth God" (1 John 4:7).

When we receive Jesus as our Saviour, we are born of God. When we are born of God we become partakers of His divine nature. God is love, so we partake of His love. That makes us love God, and it enables us to love people. We can even love those that we do not find particularly likable.

God expressed His love for the lost by giving His only begotten Son to die on a cross. Jesus expressed His love by willingly going to the cross and dying. We can express our love by giving ourselves in service to others. We especially show our love when we pray for others and endeavor to win them to Christ.

Jesus tells us to love our enemies and to do good to those who hate us (Luke 6:27). We can only love our enemies by the imparted love of God. In Romans 5:5 we are told, *". . . the love of God is shed abroad in our hearts by the Holy Ghost which is given unto us."* That imparted love binds us to the family of God, and it is an evidence that we are children of God.

January 26

The Treasure of the Heart

"A good man out of the good treasure of his heart bringeth forth that which is good; and an evil man out of the evil treasure of his heart bringeth forth that which is evil: for of the abundance of the heart his mouth speaketh" (Luke 6:45).

A treasure is something that people store and keep. Thoughts, attitudes, desires, and patterns of speech are things that we store in our hearts. When we talk, out comes the treasures of our hearts. If our hearts are not right, our speech will not honor the Lord. Our speech will not honor Christ unless we fill our hearts with Christ-honoring thoughts, desires and purposes.

D. L. Moody used to say that if there were a window in front of the heart so that people could see what was inside, most people would want to cover the window with a curtain. The things we say are an open window to the things we have stored in our hearts. That is why it is so important that we fill our hearts with good thoughts, good deeds, good ambitions, and good memories. Also, we should fill our hearts with the Word of God. David wrote, *"Thy word have I hid in mine heart, that I might not sin against thee"* (Psa. 119:11).

January 27

Jesus Understands

". . . the Word was God . . . And the Word was made flesh, and dwelt among us, . . ." (John 1:1, 14).

Jesus was God, and He became man. He was born of a woman. He became flesh and dwelt among us. He had the experience of growing from babyhood to manhood. He endured trials, temptations, and suffering. He faced difficulties. He endured the pain of rejection. Finally He died a shameful death by crucifixion.

Whatever your trials may be, He understands and cares. During His life on earth, Jesus often spoke of having compassion on people. He wept at the tomb of Lazarus, and He wept over Jerusalem. In Psalm 103:14 we read, *"For he knoweth our frame; he remembereth that we are dust."*

The Lord understands our heartaches. He knows the pain we feel. He understands our struggles. He notes our falling tears. We are told in His Word that He puts our tears in His bottle and in His book (Psa. 56:8). We should not spend time feeling sorry for ourselves. Instead, we should take our burdens to the Lord, and we should be thankful that He understands and cares.

January 28

Forgiving Others

"But if ye forgive not men their trespasses, neither will your Father forgive your trespasses" (Matt. 6:15).

We cannot afford to be unforgiving. Holding a

grudge is self-destructive. Pent-up anger destroys peace of mind, poisons the disposition, and undermines health. To avoid reaping the results of an unforgiving spirit, the transgression must be forgiven and put out of mind.

Saying, "I will forgive, but I won't forget" is a subterfuge. That is not forgiveness at all. Of course the cause of the hard feelings cannot be entirely forgotten, but it can be remembered without malice. The one who caused the break in fellowship must again be received as a friend and treated like one. Only then can you have peace of mind.

If we are not willing to forgive others, we have no right to expect God to forgive us. That does not mean loss of salvation, it does mean loss of fellowship with God. That is a price we should not be willing to pay. It is bad enough to lose fellowship with a friend; to lose fellowship with God is intolerable.

January 29

Joy in the Lord

". . . we also joy in God through our Lord Jesus Christ, by whom we have now received the atonement" (Rom. 5:11).

Many have believed the devil's lie that Christians are not supposed to enjoy life. To them being a Christian means adhering to a lot of "Thou shalt not" commandments. That is often interpreted to mean, "Thou shalt not enjoy life." That is not true, but there are professed Christians who help Satan promote the idea by spreading gloom and despair.

We should remember that Jesus was an exciting personality. Crowds thronged Him wherever He went. Even little children climbed into His arms. He once compared Himself and His disciples to a wedding party. He also spoke of His joy and wanted His joy to be in His followers.

People are not saved by being joyful, but when they receive salvation, joy comes along with it. Christians have the privilege of being joyful and of letting others know that it is a happy experience to serve the Lord.

We have to stay close to the Lord to have His joy. Sin will rob us of our joy. When King David sinned he lost his joy. He prayed for forgiveness, for cleansing, and for the restoration of his lost joy. He knew that only then would he be able to win others to the Lord (Psa. 51:12, 13).

January 30

Praying Through Depression

"I will sing unto the LORD, because he hath dealt bountifully with me" (Psa. 13:6).

King David must have been having a bad time, judging from his prayer recorded in Psalm 13. He thought that God had forgotten him and was hiding His face from him. His heart was filled with sorrow every day, and his enemy was getting the best of him. He was even afraid he was going to die.

In his troubles, he cried out to God. He prayed through the fog that clouded his vision. He prayed until his doubts were gone. He remembered that God had saved him and remembered the blessings God had given him. Then he started rejoicing. His prayer brought had him from doubt to deliverance and from sadness to singing.

We all have our dark days. When such days come it is easy to forget the blessings of God. That is when we need to cry out to God until the storm clouds lift and the rainbow of promise spans our sky.

January 31

Handfuls on Purpose

"And let fall also some of the handfuls of purpose for her, and leave them, that she may glean them, and rebuke her not" (Ruth 2:16).

Ruth was a poor Moabite widow, a stranger in Israel. Besides that, she was a hated Gentile. She had journeyed with her widowed mother-in-law from Moab to Bethlehem. They had arrived penniless and destitute. Soon Ruth went, as the poor were allowed to do, to glean in a barley field to provide food for them to eat.

Ruth started gleaning in the field of a wealthy landowner named Boaz. He saw her and told his reapers to drop handfuls of barley on purpose for her. According to the law of the day, the poor were allowed to pick up such grain as the harvesters accidentally dropped. In most cases there must have been little for the poor to collect, but Ruth was given handfuls on purpose.

Ruth was not given handfuls on purpose without reason. She could have stayed in Moab, but she had chosen to follow her mother-in-law and to worship her mother-in-law's God. She had chosen to reap in the field of Boaz, a type of Christ. That means that she was gleaning in the field of the Master, and the Master provided handfuls on purpose for her.

Those of us who have chosen to receive Jesus as our Saviour and to work faithfully in His harvest field also have handfuls of blessings dropped for us on purpose. We have only to claim them.

Devotions for February

February 1

Blessings Beyond Measure

"Honour the LORD with thy substance, and with the firstfruits of all thine increase: So shall thy barns be filled with plenty, and thy presses shall burst out with new wine" (Prov. 3:9, 10).

Some of God's promises are conditional. His promise of material blessing is one of them. In our text He promises to bless those who honor Him with what they own and with what they earn. When we give of our material possessions, God has promised to bless us with material blessings. In Luke 6:38 we are told, *"Give, and it shall be given unto you; good measure, pressed down, and shaken together, and running over, shall men give into your bosom. . . ."*

God never experiences hard times. His bank never fails. His ships never break up on the rocks or get lost in a fog. His blessings are never in short supply. He has promised to bless us when we meet His conditions, and we know that He will keep His promise.

Sometimes God delivers His blessings in strange ways. Ravenous, black-winged birds brought food to Elijah in the wilderness. Bees put honey in a dead lion for Samson. A widow fed Elijah from an empty cruse of oil and an empty meal barrel. Jesus fed a multitude with a little boy's lunch. Adversity sometimes brings blessings, and the swift dove of God's blessing often swoops down to meet our needs when least expected.

February 2

Blessed Forgiveness

"And David said unto Nathan, I have sinned against the LORD. And Nathan said unto David, The LORD also hath put away thy sin . . ." (2 Sam. 12:13).

Our text deals with three things: 1. It deals with David's sins; 2. It deals with his confession; and 3. It deals with God's forgiveness. David had sinned greatly. He had sinned against his position as king. He had sinned against Israel. He had sinned against Uriah and his wife, Bathsheba, and he had sinned against God. Like many today, he did not repent until his sin was discovered. He did not say, *"I have sinned against the Lord"* until the prophet Nathan said, *"Thou art the man."* David had sinned greatly, but God forgave him when he confessed.

God forgives the sins of His children today when they confess them. It is when we hide our sins that we run into trouble. The Bible tells us, "He *that covereth his sins shall not prosper: but whoso confesseth and forsaketh them shall have mercy"* (Prov. 28:13). That wonderful verse in 1 John 1:9 says, *"If we confess our sins, he is faithful and just to forgive us our sins, and to cleanse us from all unrighteousness."*

God has forgiveness for us today just as He did in the past. We can still come into His presence and confess our sins. Our part is to confess our sins. God's part is to forgive our sins so we can walk with Him in blessed fellowship.

February 3

Having Fellowship With God

"Draw nigh to God, and he will draw nigh to you . . ." (James 4:8).

We can sense the presence of God when we wait before Him in prayer, but this is not easy in our rushing workaday lives. More often than not we drop on our knees and utter our usual brief prayer with no sense whatever of the presence of God. It takes time to commune with God.

Another way we can draw near to God is by reading, searching, and memorizing His Word. Reading the Bible is like mining for gold. There are precious promises that we may have overlooked in previous readings. There are other times when a passage or a verse seems to leap from the page, and we know that it is God's promise for us. When that happens we should claim the promise and make it our own.

We can also draw near to God by leaning upon Him. We need His wisdom, His guidance, and His power. Most of all we need the assurance of His presence.

February 4

Our Wilderness Journey

"These all died in faith . . . and confessed that they were strangers and pilgrims on the earth" (Heb. 11:13).

In this chapter the writer calls the honor roll of people who lived by faith in the past. They made life's journey as pilgrims and strangers. We have to make the journey in the same way. We are not citizens of this world. We are citizens of Heaven (Phil. 3:20). See the reference in the center column of the Scofield Bible.

We are not simply on a journey from the cradle to the grave; we are on a journey from conception to eternity. We are traveling through hostile territory on our way. The world hates us as it hated our Saviour, so we must walk the pathway of life by faith.

On this journey we are ambassadors for Christ. (2 Cor. 5:20). An ambassador is a representative of his government in a foreign country. As ambassadors, we represent Christ. We must live like citizens of Heaven, and we are to endeavor to lead others to receive the Lord Jesus Christ as their Saviour. To be a true ambassador for Christ, we must walk with Him by faith.

February 5

Triumph Over Trials

". . . there was given to me a thorn in the flesh, the messenger of Satan to buffet me, lest I should be exalted above measure" (2 Cor. 12:7).

Paul's thorn in his flesh must have been painful. He prayed three times for God to remove it, but God did not remove it. Instead, God gave him sufficient grace to bear the thorn. Paul learned that a painful thorn can serve a purpose. He came to realize that God allowed his thorn to keep him from being puffed up.

I once told a doctor about a person who had succeeded in spite of a severe handicap. The doctor remarked that the person probably succeeded because of the handicap. History is replete with examples of people who have succeeded in spite of handicaps.

Thomas Edison, the great inventor, was deaf. Fanny Crosby, the matchless songwriter, was blind.

Isaac Watts, poet and writer of 697 hymns, was sickly. William Cowper, famous hymn writer and poet, was melancholy. Alexander Cruden, writer of the first complete Bible concordance, was mentally ill. Jacob, the son of Isaac, was lame. Having a weakness or a disability does not mean that we cannot do worthwhile things. Paul recognized this principle and wrote, ". . . *when I am weak, then am I strong"* (2 Cor. 12:10). When we have trials we should not give up. Instead we should do even more for God.

February 6

Precepts to Live By

"BE not thou envious against evil men, neither desire to be with them" (Prov. 24:1).

The first part of this proverb has to do with attitude. Christians should never have the wrong attitude toward sinful people. We should not envy them when they prosper or when they appear to be enjoying life. Instead, we should feel sorry for them. They are having the only good times they will ever have. In eternity they will only have suffering. On the other hand, Christians are now having the worst time they will ever have. In eternity Christians will have glory and blessings beyond description. The second thing in this proverb is about relationships. We should not become intimate friends with sinful people, and we should not spend a great deal of time with them. We can attempt to win them to Christ, but we should not be deceived into thinking that we can convert them by becoming close friends with them. Remember the old adage, "One rotten apple will spoil a bushel of good apples."

February 7

Walk the Walk

"That ye might walk worthy of the Lord . . . being fruitful in every good work, and increasing in the knowledge of God" (Col. 1:10).

Today we have the catch phrase that says, "Walk the walk." That is a good idea. We should never live beneath the profession we make. An even better phrase would be, "Talk the talk, and walk the walk." In other words saved people ought to talk like Christians and they should walk like Christians. Our lives should be a testimony for the Lord every day.

We need to increase in the knowledge of God and be fruitful in good works. We can increase our knowledge of God by reading and studying His Word, and we can learn more about God by associating with godly people. We can learn much from those who walk intimately with the Lord. We can also learn by attending a church where a godly pastor preaches the Word of God. Being active in such a church will offer opportunities to become involved in good works, and that will help us to "Walk the walk."

February 8

Power to Witness

"But ye shall receive power, after that the Holy Ghost is come upon you: and ye shall be witnesses unto me . . ." (Acts 1:8).

Our heavenly Father is a God of power. In the beginning He filled limitless space with blazing stars and whirling planets, and He made the beautiful world in which we live. He holds the winds in His fists and the mighty oceans in the hollow of His hand. In the springtime He paints the flowers with all the colors of the rainbow. All about us are evidences of the loving care of the God who created the universe. Our Saviour now has all power in Heaven and on earth, and He has promised to empower us through the Holy Spirit. Primarily this is power to win souls, but it is also power to live victoriously. We cannot live victoriously in our own strength, but we can have victory through Christ. Paul wrote, *"I can do all things through Christ which strengtheneth me"* (Phil. 4:13). We have the same Christ that Paul had, and He can strengthen us just as He strengthened Paul.

Through Christ we can conquer temptations and overcome difficulties. He is able to give us victory in spite of our weaknesses. He can enable us to accomplish more than we ever thought possible. Things of earth may hinder, but Christ can give us victory. By faith we can accomplish things that are far-and-away beyond our own ability. Claim His power and blessing, and have a fruitful and victorious day.

February 9

Showers of Blessings

". . . I will cause the shower to come down in his season; there shall be showers of blessing" (Ezek. 34:26).

Seasons are not always the same. There are dry seasons, cold seasons, hot seasons, and wet seasons. Some of the seasons are unpleasant, even harsh, but God makes them all work for our good.

When you have to go through a bad season, take heart. God has promised showers of blessings. Notice that showers is plural. You just have to believe and wait for God to bring the season of blessings your way. When dark clouds cover your sky, remember that they have a silver lining.

C. H. Spurgeon wrote, "Look up today, O parched spirit, and open thy leaves and flowers for a heavenly watering."

The poet, Longfellow, wrote:

> Be still sad heart and cease repining.
> Behind the cloud the sun's still shining.
> Thy fate is the common fate of all.
> Into each life some rain must fall.

God is still on the throne. The sun is still shining, and the showers of blessings will come again in due season.

February 10
God Is with Us

"... *I am with you, saith the LORD*" (Hag. 1:13).

One night at the beginning of a service, I heard the great evangelist, Gypsy Smith, say, "I have walked with the Lord intimately for many years. I feel His presence tonight, and He is well pleased with the service."

It is said that when John Wesley was dying he said, "The best of all, God is with us."

You do not have to be well-known to be aware of the presence of the Lord. His promises are for all His children. We can all enjoy His presence and His blessings. Even when we are going through storms, He is with us. His presence can be more real than that at other times.

Are you lonely, discouraged, or troubled. Take heart. God is with you.

I Trust In God

I do not walk my way by sight,
Nor do I fear the coming night.
Though the future is unknown,
I trust in God alone,
For He is on the throne.

—Louis Arnold

February 11

Ours Is the Victory

"Now thanks be unto God, which always causeth us to triumph in Christ . . ." (2 Cor. 2:14).

The Apostle Paul had been through great trials, yet he wrote that we can always triumph in Christ. He had known arrests, imprisonments, scourgings, stonings, shipwrecks, and more, but he remained confident.

God does not give us a miracle when we do not need a miracle If He demonstrated His power with every change of the wind, we would not have to walk by faith. We must believe that God is present even when we are going through a dark valley. The fourth man, like unto the Son of God, did not walk with the three Hebrew children until they were cast into the fire of the furnace. That was when they needed Him, and that was when He walked with them.

Some of the most victorious people are those who were going through the greatest trials. A man I visited who was confined to his bed by crippling arthritis gave a glowing testimony to all who entered his room. A lady I visited on her deathbed had a shining face, a glowing smile, and an encouraging word for all who entered her room. A lady I knew who had gone through repeated operations for brain tumors memorized much of the Bible and delighted to recite passages to everyone who came near her. Truly God gives victory when it is needed.

February 12
Giving Heed to Opportunity

"THEREFORE we ought to give the more earnest heed to the things which we have heard, lest at any time we should let them slip" (Heb. 2:1).

They say that opportunity knocks only once, but that is not true when it comes to being saved and serving the Lord. Opportunity to be saved knocks on the heart's door of the unsaved again and again, but there comes a time when it knocks for the last time. Opportunity to be involved in the Lord's work also comes again and again, but when we do not act the opportunity will slip away. We should give heed to our opportunities today.

Unsaved people can let opportunity after opportunity to be saved slip by. If they continue on that road, one day the last opportunity will slip away and they will never be saved.

The river of opportunity flows before the saved every day. If we only watch the river run past, we will never do the work God wants us to do. Once we know the will of God, we should plunge in and give our best in His service.

There is a line by us unseen
That crosses every path,
The hidden boundary between
God's mercy and His wrath.
—Author Unknown

February 13

Musing

"My heart was hot within me, while I was musing the fire burned . . ." (Psa. 39:3).

King David sat before an open fire thinking. He thought of his frailties and of the shortness of life—and he prayed. Most of us consider eternal values in thoughtful moments.

We now live in the early years of the twenty-first century. Behind us are the dimming mists of past history, and before that prehistoric ages are obscured and muddied by the uncertain conjectures of science. But, we are not to be discouraged. We have the light of revelation. *"In the beginning God created . . ."*

From the day of creation the stream of humanity has flowed through the ages, ever widening until the present hour. That stream parts at a cross and becomes two streams, one larger than the other. The streams have flowed through darkness, storms, troubles and wars, and always a guiding light has pointed the way for those in the smaller stream.

Looking to the future, one stream of humanity will flow into the abyss. The other stream, clear as crystal and bright as polished silver, will flow into the glorious light of the presence of God. God grant that in your musings you have that hope of eternal morning.

February 14

Rejoice in the Lord

"REJOICE in the LORD, O ye righteous: for praise is comely [fitting, pleasing, and beautiful] for the upright" (Psa. 33:1).

It is good to start the day with rejoicing. Even

when we have troubles, trials, sickness, or sorrow, we should rejoice in the Lord. It is a blessing to be alive. It is great to have loved ones and friends, and it is wonderful to be saved. *"REJOICE in the Lord . . ."* Jesus is our Saviour. God is our Father. The church is our sphere of activity. Saved people are our brothers and sisters. We have the privilege of prayer, and we have the privilege of working for God. We are on our way to Heaven. *"REJOICE in the Lord . . ."*

When you have a bad day, whining and complaining will only make matters worse. When your spirits are low, feeling sorry for yourself will make you feel worse. Change your mind and your attitude. Look for things to be thankful for, and *"REJOICE in the Lord . . ."*

February 15

Comforting Truth

"But now he is dead . . . I shall go to him, but he shall not return to me" (2 Sam. 12:23).

King David's child had died, and he comforted himself with the thought that one day he would see his child again. The following illustration may be of comfort to those who have lost loved ones.

One Sunday afternoon, years ago, I flew in a chartered plane from Lexington, Kentucky to Cincinnati, Ohio to help organize a church. That was my first trip in a plane, and I found that I had to exercise a good deal of faith on the flight. I had to believe that the plane could fly, and I had to believe that the pilot knew how to fly it. But that was not the end of my faith. From the moment we took off, I was hopelessly lost, and I had to trust the pilot to find the way.

Near the end of our flight, I saw the Ohio River flowing down a valley. Beyond the river I saw the skyline of Cincinnati. We would have to cross the river to reach the city, and when we did, I would be separated from loved ones I had left at home. Beyond the river friends were waiting for me. Soon I would be with them the other side of the river, and I would be busy for my Lord there. That brought to my mind the river that I will one day cross to the City of God, and it made Heaven seem very real and very near.

What a comfort it is to know that the loved ones we have lost are in the City of God and that one day we will join them as I was now going to join my friends beyond the Ohio River.

February 16
Bearing the Burdens of Others

"Bear ye one another's burdens, and so fulfil the law of Christ" (Gal. 6:2).

Paul tells us that we fulfill the law of Christ when we bear one another's burdens. The Apostle John quotes Christ saying, *"A new commandment I give unto you, That ye love one another; as I have loved you . . ."* (John 13:34). Loving others makes it easy to share their burdens.

In an earlier day in our country, when we were not pressured and hurried as we are today, it was the general practice for neighbor to help neighbor. Even unsaved people helped their friends in times of need. We need to return to that practice. Especially those who love the Lord should bear the burdens of others.

Christ loved us and bore our sins on the cross. If we love others as He loved us, we will gladly share their burdens. There is no better way to be a living testimony than by bearing the burdens of others.

There is no better way to share the burdens of the unsaved than to lead them to trust Christ as Saviour and to let Him bear their burdens.

February 17
The Value of Small Things

"And through a window in a basket was I let down by the wall, and escaped his hands" (2 Cor. 11:33).

Paul was saved from capture and possible death by a rope. His friends used a rope to lower him from a window in a basket. His great ministry would not have been possible without that rope. Moses was preserved in a small, handmade ark. John Wesley was saved from a burning house when he was a child. Two peasants formed a ladder and rescued him from an upstairs window. God uses small things.

A sailor swam from a sinking ship to a Pacific island that was inhabited by cannibals. He carried ashore the Bible his mother had given him. Sixty years later a British ship stopped at the island and found churches, schools, and homes. That was because of the Bible the sailor had carried ashore. If the sailor had dropped the Bible in the ocean the people on the island would still have been cannibals.

Small decisions often alter the future of an individual or a family beyond anything expected. That it why it is so important to seek God's leading in all that we do. God wants to bless us, and His greatest blessings are found in the center of His will.

February 18
Working for Jesus

". . . God hath chosen the weak things of the world to confound the things which are mighty" (1 Cor. 1:27).

God will use anyone who is willing to be used, and He often calls those who are not willing into His service. Moses is one such example.

Moses was a most unlikely prospect for the Lord's work. As a young man he had attempted to better the lives of his kinsmen in Egypt and had failed. He killed an Egyptian in the attempt, then fled for his life. For forty years he lived on the backside of the desert and did nothing more important than herd sheep that did not belong to him. He married a woman who was not an Israelite. That was something God had forbidden. Moses was further handicapped by being slow of speech, and he lacked self-confidence.

When God called him to return to Egypt and deliver His people, he refused to go and asked God to send someone else. Yet, despite all this, when Moses finally obeyed the Lord, he became a great leader. He is considered the greatest of the prophets, and he became the greatest lawgiver of all time.

The God who used Moses will use anyone who is willing to be used. Today is the first day of the rest of your life. Let it be the day when you surrender to do the will of God.

February 19

Blessed Assurance

"The Spirit itself beareth witness with our spirit, that we are the children of God" (Rom. 8:16).

One way to have assurance of salvation is to take God at His Word. For example, Jesus tells us that if we will come to Him He will not turn us away (John 6:37). When we come to Jesus and trust Him to save us, we can claim His promises. Thus we can know that we are saved. There are many passages in the Bible that serve the same purpose.

Another way we can know that we are saved is by the witness of the Holy Spirit. The Spirit bears witness with our spirit that we are the children of God, and that witness brings a feeling of peace and confidence. We are not saved by feelings, but knowing that we are saved does give us a good feeling. Even when we do not feel well, the peace of God abides with us. By faith we can know we are saved whether we feel like it or not. By faith we can be as sure of Heaven as we will be when we get there. Knowing that we are saved will enable us to live victoriously and to be a blessing to others.

February 20

Needed Light

"For thou wilt light my candle: the LORD my God will enlighten my darkness" (Psa. 18:28).

The Psalmist wrote of going through darkness, then added, *"For thou wilt light my candle. . . ."* That was a statement of faith. While still in darkness, he was trusting God for light.

We walk by faith, but, even so, there are times when our sun of hope appears to go down, and we feel as if we are walking in a fog without the light of a single star. At such times the light of a candle would help, and God has promised to light our candle. As God gave light to the Psalmist in his time of darkness, He will surely give light to us.

A candle has only a tiny flame, but it can light one's way in darkness. It does not take great faith to claim such a tiny flame from the God who commanded the light to shine in the morning of creation. The tiny light of the candle can be a faith-builder, and it can lead to the light of blessings as yet unseen. Trust God to light your candle and to make you a light-bearer for others.

February 21

Victory Through God's Word

"Thy word have I hid in mine heart, that I might not sin against thee" (Psa. 119:11).

The 119th Psalm is unique. All but 3 of its 176 verses refer to the Word of God. The Word of God is referred to as the law, the way of the Lord, His precepts, His statutes, His commandments, His righteous judgments, His Word and so forth.

This Psalm is unique in its structure. It has been called the Alphabet Psalm. It is divided into 22 divisions of 8 verses each. The first 8 verses begin with the first letter of the Hebrew alphabet, the second with the second letter and so on through the entire Hebrew alphabet. That means that no matter how you spell it, the Word of God is there to help. We can hide the Word of God in our hearts to give us strength to say no when temptation comes.

In the New Testament Jesus tells us that He is the first and last letters of the Greek alphabet (Rev. 1:8). He is the living Word of God, and He is everything we need in the earthly journey. The alphabet is all we need to spell every word in the dictionary, and Jesus is all we need to give meaning to all of life.

February 22

Dwelling at Bethel

"AND God said unto Jacob, Arise, go up to Beth-el, and dwell there: and make there an altar unto God, that appeared unto thee . . ." (Gen. 35:1).

Bethel means the house of God. After years of disobedience, Jacob was commanded to go to Bethel, to dwell there, and to make an altar there. It was to be his place of residence and his place of worship.

Years before Jacob had cheated his brother, Esau, out of his birthright and his blessing. Esau became so angry Jacob had to flee for his life. The first night away from home he slept at Bethel. That night he had seen a vision of angels ascending and descending a ladder that reached to Heaven. He recognized the presence of God, but he did not tarry there. Instead he went on to Haran, the place of halfway obedience. That was where Abraham stopped halfway on his journey to Canaan.

Jacob dwelt in Haran for a number of years. That was not the place of God's choosing, yet God blessed him there. Even so, he had to endure great hardships. At last God spoke to Jacob and told him to go to Bethel, the place of complete obedience. There God could bless him as he had not blessed him before.

We too can stop at a place of halfway obedience. God may bless us there, but we will have to pay a price for being out of His will. God's greatest blessings are only available in the place of His choosing. Each of us should go to our Bethel and dwell there. There, God will bless us in ways we never dreamed possible.

February 23

Victory over Trials

"Beloved, think it not strange concerning the fiery trial which is to try you . . ." (1 Pet. 4:12).

It is not unusual for people to suffer or to have trials in this life. Because sin is in the world, suffering and sorrow are in the world. The Bible tells us that

"MAN . . . is of few days and full of trouble" (Job 14:1).

All about us are people who are going through fiery trials. Many of them are Christians. They groan in pain in this life, but they will shout the victory in eternity.

When trials come our way we should bear them patiently. Whining and whimpering only makes us feel worse, and it makes those around us miserable. We should not spread our misery even if we do have enough to share with others.

When we are tried, we should draw near to the Lord and trust Him for victory. Our attitude during trial will often determine the outcome. Trials can wear us down or they can make us grow stronger. No matter what goes wrong, keep on *"Looking unto Jesus the author and finisher of our faith . . ."* (Heb. 12:2).

February 24

Dealing With Fear

". . . Fear not; I will help thee" (Isa. 41:13).

It is human to fear. Children often cry out in fear when there is no cause for fear. In their fear they want someone to comfort them. The strong, loving arms of a parent will usually quiet them and make them forget their fear.

Our heavenly Father knows that we have fears, and He wants to comfort us and give us victory over them. Throughout the Bible we find the phrase, *"Fear not,"* again and again. In our text God not only told the people of Israel not to fear, He promised to help them. Surely God will help His children today just as He helped Israel in Old Testament days.

We often fear the unknown. When we do it is well to remember that there is nothing unknown to God. When we cannot find our way, He can direct us. When we cannot find the solution to a problem, He can show us the solution. When we have problems with others, God can help us face the problems with a Christian spirit, and He can give us grace to pray for those who despitefully use us.

February 25

Pleasing God

"By faith Enoch was translated that he should not see death . . . But without faith it is impossible to please him: for he that cometh to God must believe that he is, and that he is a rewarder of them that diligently seek him" (Heb. 11:5, 6).

In Genesis 5:22 we are told that Enoch walked with God. His walk started by faith and continued by faith. We also should walk with God. To begin the walk with God we must believe that God exists. To continue the walk with Him we must believe that He rewards those who diligently seek Him.

Our text tells us that we cannot please God without faith. Enoch believed God and walked with Him. We too can believe God and walk with Him. We can live victoriously, just as Enoch did, and we to can have a testimony that we are pleasing God.

When we please God, He will answer our prayers. In 1 John 3:22 we are told that God will answer our prayers if we keep His commandments and do things that are pleasing in His sight. The walk of faith is the walk of victory. God rewards those who walk by faith and live to serve and please Him.

February 26

Steps to Victory

"Delight thyself also in the LORD; and he shall give thee the desires of thine heart" (Psa. 37:4).

This is a tremendous verse from a superb chapter. The chapter begins by telling us not to worry and continues by giving us steps to victory. These steps are like climbing a stairway. Verse 3 gives us two steps. Step one is, *"Trust in the Lord."* Step two is, *"Do good."* Verse 4 gives us step three. It is, *"Delight thyself also in the LORD."* Verse 5 gives us step four. *"Commit thy way unto the LORD."* We take step five in verse 7. There we reach the top of the stairs where we, *"Rest in the LORD."*

Our text is the pivotal verse in this Psalm. The things we delight in shows the index to our soul. We cannot commit our way to the Lord without first delighting in Him.

When we delight in things that are displeasing to the Lord, He has not promised to give us the desires of our heart. We must bring our desires into subjection to the Lord's will and delight in Him before we can claim this promise. May God help you to climb the steps to victory today.

February 27

When Alone and in Need

"And Jacob was left alone; and there wrestled a man with him until the breaking of the day . . . And he said, I will not let thee go, except thou bless me" (Gen. 32:24, 26).

Jacob was alone. It was night; he was in trouble, and he wrestled all night with an unnamed man. That must have been the longest, darkest night of his life. Finally, with the breaking of dawn, he claimed the blessing that changed his life.

Jacob's experience was a picture of wrestling in prayer. The unnamed man was perhaps an angel or the Lord Himself. Whoever the man was, he had the power to make Jacob lame. That meant that he was never again as strong as he had been before that night, and he was more dependent upon the Lord than before. His name was changed, and he was changed. After that trying night, he was a better servant of the Lord than he had ever been before.

Others have gone through long, lonely, trying nights. They too have wrestled with an adversary that was too strong for them. They too have called out for a blessing when it seemed that the dawning of a new day would never come. They too have found victory when it seemed there was no way of victory, and their trials made them better servants of the Lord. Trials can be stepping-stones instead of stumbling blocks.

February 28

Bitter Sweet

"How shall we sing the LORD'S song in a strange land?" (Psa. 137:4).

The people of Israel were exiled in far-off Babylon. Memories of home filled their hearts with sorrow. They lost their song, and they hung their idle harps upon the willow trees. Their captors mocked them, saying, *". . . Sing us one of the songs of Zion."* They replied, *"How shall we sing the LORD'S song in a strange land?"* This is a text that gets hold of our heartstrings.

Mingled with the memories of happy days in their old home, there were memories of their sins and of God's judgment. Sin had placed them in their present estate, and the only way back their former joy was to get right with God. When they finally did get right with God, He turned again their captivity. They were allowed to go home, and their mouths were filled with laughter and singing (Psa. 126:1, 2).

Like the people of Israel, we lose our joy when we harbor unconfessed and unforgiven sins, and like them, we can regain our joy when we confess and forsake our sins. God wants us to be close to Him, and when we are, like ancient Israel, our mouths can be filled with laughter and our tongues with singing.

February 29

Reasons for Being Thankful

O GIVE thanks unto the LORD; call upon his name: make known his deeds among the people (Psa. 105:1).

It has been four years since the last leap year. We should be thankful that God has let us live another four years. Another reason for being thankful is the privilege of prayer. Our Scripture tells us to call upon the name of the Lord. It is awesome that we can come into the presence of God and make known our requests to Him. The text gives us yet another reason for being thankful. We should be thankful that we can tell others about the great things God has done for us.

Devotions for March

March 1

The Power of a Soft Answer

*"A SOFT answer turneth away wrath: but griev-
ous words stir up anger"* (Prov. 15:1).

"Blessed are the peacemakers . . ." (Matt. 5:9).

It is not easy to control anger when we are
misused, put upon, or spoken to harshly, or unkindly.
At such times it is well to remember that it takes two
to make an argument. Your assailant is at a
disadvantage when you answer gently, kindly, or
sweetly.

A perfectly beautiful day can be spoiled by a
senseless argument. Hurt feelings can result and they
can linger long after the cause of the misunderstanding
is forgotten. It is more sensible and more Christian
to avoid the argument in the first place by answering
softly. The soft answer can turn away anger, and make
it possible for both parties to laugh over a silly
misunderstanding.

The peacemaker is a blessed person. That means
that the peacemaker is blessed of God. Nowhere in
the Bible is there a promise of blessings to
troublemakers. They make others unhappy, and they
make themselves miserable.

Decide to make each day a good day, and that
you will love others and get along with them.

March 2

God Knows

"*. . . Lord, thou knowest all things; thou knowest that I love thee . . .*" (John 21:17).

The cross and the tomb were behind Jesus, and He was having one of His last meetings with His disciples before going back to His Father. Three times He asked Peter if he loved Him, and three times Peter avowed that he did. Finally, perhaps a bit exasperated, Peter exclaimed, "*. . . Lord thou knowest all things; thou knowest that I love thee.*"

Jesus does know all things. He knows all things from creation's dawn to eternity's glory. He knew when Peter followed Him afar off. He knew when Peter warmed himself at the enemies' fire. He knew each time Peter denied Him. He knew when Peter cursed and swore. He knew when Peter went out and wept. He knew all about Peter, and still He loved him.

He knows all about each of us. He knows our shortcomings, yet He loves us. He knows our trials. He sees the falling tear. The Saviour who wept with Martha and Mary at the tomb of their brother, Lazarus, cares about each of us. We can take comfort that He knows and still loves us. How comforting that, no matter what our past, and no matter what our present may be, He loves us, and we can go boldly to the throne of grace and find forgiveness, comfort, and guidance.

March 3

Where to Fly From Trouble

"*And I said, Oh that I had wings like a dove! for then would I fly away, and be at rest*" (Psa. 55:6).

There are times when most of us wish we could go away and leave our troubles behind. The problem with that wish is that we would take most of our troubles with us. We would take our memories with us, and that would be trouble enough. Also, we would take our personality quirks with us, and we would still have to live with ourselves.

There is something better than flying away like a dove. Instead, we should fly to the almighty arms of our heavenly Father. It is said that Charles Wesley, the brother of the great preacher, John Wesley, and a great songwriter in his own right, was on board a ship during a violent storm. While on deck, possibly tied in place to keep from being washed overboard, a small bird, driven before the storm, took refuge in his coat. Based on that experience, when the storm was over he wrote the great song:

Jesus Lover of My Soul

Jesus, Lover of my soul,
Let me to Thy bosom fly;
While the nearer waters roll,
While the tempest still is high.
Hide me, O my Savior hide,
Till the storm of life is past;
Safe into the haven guide,
O receive my soul at last.

March 4

Past Faith

"But we trusted [past tense] *. . . O fools, and slow of heart to believe all that the prophets have spoken"* (Luke 24:21, 25).

How touching, how full of meaning is this passage

from Luke. Jesus had risen from the dead, but the disciples were confused and doubtful. Two of them were walking to Emmaus, a village a little more than 7 miles from Jerusalem. They were heavyhearted, and they talked of all that had happened. Jesus joined them in their walk, but they did not recognize Him. He asked them why they were troubled, and they told Him of Jesus and His crucifixion. They told how they had trusted that He would redeem Israel. How sad that they could not say. "We are still trusting, even though everything seems to be against us."

We must learn to trust even when we cannot see the light at the end of the tunnel. Things we believed yesterday are not sufficient for the present. We must have faith for today. It takes little faith to sail on a calm sea. A howling tempest is the real test of our faith.

Faith for Today

Lord give me faith so strong
It will last my whole life long.
Even when my sky is gray,
Help me, Lord to trust and pray.
Direct me with Your guiding hand
As I journey through this land.

—Louis Arnold

March 5
How to Face Trials

"Then they cried unto the LORD in their trouble, and he delivered them out of their distresses" (Psa. 107:6).

Trials are meant to be stepping-stones, but they can become stumbling blocks instead. Stepping-stones can lead us up the path of light to a higher plain, or we can stumble over them and be broken.

What we do about our trials depends upon our attitude. We can look on the dark side and bewail our fate, or we can look to the Lord in faith and know that He will work out His will for us. We can go through life expecting the worst, or we can look to God and expect His blessings. We usually get what we expect. We must learn to walk by faith and enjoy the blessings of God each day.

When trials come, we can rejoice that we do not have to bear them alone. The Lord wants to be our light in darkness, our strength in weakness, and our comfort in sorrow. When trials come we should recognize His presence and cast our care upon Him.

March 6

Surrender to God's Will

"... *not my will, but thine, be done*" (Luke 22:42).

Under the shadow of death, with the agony and horror of the cross facing Him, Jesus prayed that God would take away the cup of suffering and death. That was the human side of Jesus dreading what He was facing. Before He tasted death for us, He tasted the dread of death. Jesus had victory, even in that hour. He prayed *"not my will, but thine be done."* There is often a conflict between our will and God's will. It is human to want to do our own thing, but the thing we want to do may not be pleasing to God. There lies the conflict.

We must remember that God's will is best. Out of His will, we cannot claim His blessings. Out of His will, we do not have His guidance. Without His guidance we must use our own judgment or depend upon the advice of friends. Our judgment may not be sufficient, and the advice of friends may not be good advice. God's leading is always right. He never leads us to make the wrong choice.

Out of God's will, we do not have His comfort. When sorrow comes, as it surely will, we will have to bear it alone. Out of God's will we are subject to temptation. Out of His will, we are in danger. Out of God's will, we run into problems. Let us draw near to Him and follow where He leads. Our prayer should always be, *". . . not my will, but thine be done."*

March 7

Serving the Invisible God

". . . though now ye see him not, yet believing, ye rejoice with joy unspeakable and full of glory" (1 Pet. 1:8).

"Now unto the King eternal, immortal, invisible, the only wise God, be honour and glory for ever and ever. Amen" (1 Tim. 1:17).

It should not trouble us that God is invisible. One day we will see Him, but for the present He chooses to be invisible. If we could see Him we would not have to walk by faith. Even though we do not see Him, by faith we can rejoice with joy unspeakable and full of glory (1 Pet. 1:8).

Many things are invisible, but that does not make us doubt their existence. Wind is invisible, but we feel it blow upon our bodies. We see it sweep across waving fields of grain, and we see it push sailboats over tossing waves. We see birds, and kites, and planes ride upon the wind, and we know that it exists.

In the same way we know that God exists. We feel His presence, and we see the things He does. Most important is the evidence of changed lives. Answered prayer is another evidence that God exists. The universe God has made is another, and the myriad forms of life that are in the world provide yet more evidences of the Creator. Because God lives we look forward to the home He has prepared for us in Heaven, and while we remain in this world, we walk with Him and serve Him.

March 8

Choose the Better Light

"Behold, all ye that kindle a fire, that compass yourselves about with sparks: walk in the light of your fire, and in the sparks that ye have kindled. This shall ye have of mine hand; ye shall lie down in sorrow" (Isa. 50:11).

One can easily read this text without catching its meaning. Read it again and ponder its message. God is saying that when we find ourselves walking in darkness, we should not attempt to make our own light. Sparks from a fire we have kindled will make very poor light.

Often we seek the advice of friends, only to find that they furnish sparks for light. We can depend upon our own reason, but all too often that is only sparks. Even advice from professionals is not always trustworthy. We should turn instead to God's Word.

In Psalm 119:105 we read. *"Thy word is a lamp unto my feet, and a light unto my path."* It is never right to do wrong, even if we think it will get us out of trouble.

Our God is light. In Him is no darkness (1 John 1:5). We should walk in His light, even when we do not understand His leading. Taking the wrong path will lead to disappointment and failure.

March 9

Be Not Discouraged

". . . the soul of the people was much discouraged because of the way" (Num. 21:4).

". . . as the LORD God of thy fathers hath said unto thee; fear not, neither be discouraged" (Deut. 1:21).

Defeat follows close upon the heels of discouragement. Faith drives discouragement away.

The Israelites were discouraged because they had a difficult path to travel. We too often find the path we must follow difficult. God has not promised that we will have no trials, but He has promised that when trials beset us, He will be with us. Our strength is often too small for the journey, but God has unlimited strength.

Often we grow discouraged because of uncertainty. We simply do not know where to turn or which way to go. When that happens, we must trust in the One who knows all things. He knows the future, and He knows what we should do. When we know not which way to go, it is always right to go to God in prayer and ask Him to guide us and to give us courage.

Years ago, Dr. Bob Engle, pastor of a church in Jacksonville, Florida, grew discouraged and resigned his church. He went to Detroit with the intention of getting a job in an automobile factory.

On Sunday he attended services in the Temple Baptist Church and heard Dr. J. Frank Norris preach. His soul was set aflame, and his vision was rekindled. At once he phoned his wife and told her to tell the men of the church not to act on his resignation, because he was coming back to build the greatest church in

Jacksonville. He did return to Jacksonville, and he did build a great church.

March 10

Hope, When There Is No Hope

"And when neither sun nor stars in many days appeared, and no small tempest lay on us, all hope that we should be saved was then taken away" (Acts 27:20).

". . . there stood by me this night the angel of God . . . Saying, Fear not, Paul . . . Wherefore, sirs, be of good cheer: for I believe God . . ." (Acts 27:23-25).

These verses are taken from a chapter that describes the ordeal Paul and the others on the boat with him endured in a storm at sea. Conditions could not have been worse. Experienced sailors had done all they could to save the ship, but to no avail. They had thrown the cargo and the tackling of the ship overboard to lighten it. Then they had given up trying to control the ship and had let the wind drive it where it would. Finally all on board, except Paul, abandoned all hope of being saved, but he fasted and prayed for many days. Then he heard from Heaven. His courage returned, and he stood on the deck of the ship and shouted for all to hear, *"Be of good cheer."*

The sun did not break through the clouds; the wind did not abate, but there was hope. Paul said, *"I believe God."* When things go wrong, we need people of faith. Often they can give us hope when we think there is no hope.

March 11

Praise God When Trials Come

"Wherefore glorify ye the LORD in the fires . . ." (Isa. 24:15).

Fiery trials are not pleasant, but they refine. Being in the fire makes us better. Testimony under pressure is the best testimony of all. Those who face trials undaunted are true leaders.

Trials come in many forms. They may come as sickness that has no remedy. They may come as pain that will not go away. They may come as the loss of employment. They may come because of a slanderous tongue. They may come as sorrow over the loss of a loved one. Whatever their form, trials come to all of us. How we bear up under them marks the measure of our faith and of our relationship with God.

When we are patient in trial, we light the way for others who are being tried. How we bear our trials can, to paraphrase the words of Paul, fall out to the furtherance of the gospel (Phil. 1:12). May God help us to glorify Him on the good days and to glorify Him no less on the bad days.

March 12

God Is Able

"Now unto him that is able to do exceeding abundantly above all that we ask or think, according to the power that worketh in us" (Eph. 3:20).

God is able. That is a foundation to rest upon. There is nothing too hard for God. He is able to answer our prayers, and He is able to help us make our dreams come true. Why then do we often flounder in a sea of failure instead of climbing the mountain of success? It may be because we want God to work for us instead of letting Him work in us.

God's power is present, but He wants our cooperation. We must live for His glory, not for self exaltation. Sin in our hearts will hinder the answer to our prayers (Psa. 66:18). Doubt will keep our prayers from being answered. We must have faith. God will not use our doubt. Jesus said, *". . . According to your faith be it unto you"* (Matt. 9:29).

God's power will enable us to live godly lives, and to do the work He has for us to do. Let us thank Him, praise Him, walk with Him, and work for Him. That is the way to victorious living.

March 13

God Answers Prayer

"And it shall come to pass, that whosoever shall call on the name of the LORD shall be delivered . . ." (Joel 2:32).

Many of God's promises are based on things we can do. For example, when we receive Christ as Saviour, He saves us. When we confess our sins, He forgives us. When we call upon Him in times of trouble, He has promised to deliver us. It is ours to call upon Him. It is His to deliver.

It is strange that we are often reluctant to call upon the Lord. We try to deliver ourselves. We run to our friends for help, or we seek the advice of professionals. We only call upon the Lord when nothing else works.

God has the power and the wisdom to deliver, and He is willing to deliver. It is folly for us to depend upon ourselves when we can call upon the Lord and trust Him to deliver in His own time and way.

March 14

The Way of Victory

"Now the just shall live by faith . . ." (Heb. 10:38).

Walking by sight does not enable us to live victorious lives; walking by faith does. Without faith it is not possible to please God. We are saved through faith and kept through faith. We walk by faith, pray in faith, and have victory through faith (1 John 5:4). We are not to have faith in faith. We are to have faith in God. Our faith may be small, but our God is great. Trusting in our faith is discouraging. Looking at conditions can be even more discouraging. Thinking of our failures can only discourage us, but trusting in God can enable us to mount up on wings of victory.

God is all-powerful. He is loving, He is forgiving, and He delights to give good things to His children. We are made to walk uprightly, and our eyes easily turn upward. You can look upward today. Trust in God, and have a great day.

March 15

Ambassadors for Christ

"For our conversation (margin = citizenship) *is in heaven..."* (Phil. 3:20).

"Now then we are ambassadors for Christ, as though God did beseech you by us: we pray you in Christ's stead, be ye reconciled to God" (2 Cor. 5:20).

Unsaved people are citizens of this world. Saved people are citizens of Heaven. When we become Christians of Heaven, God does not at once take us there. Instead, He leaves us in the world as His ambassadors. That means we are in a foreign land as representatives of Heaven.

No wonder there is so much in the world of which we do not approve. Satan is the prince of this world (Eph. 2:2). Unsaved people are the children of Satan, and they do the things he wants them to do (John 8:44). That is why there is so much senseless wickedness and violence in the world.

As ambassadors, serving in Christ's place, we are to persuade people to be reconciled to God. That means that we are to win others to Christ. The love of Christ constrains us to live and work as ambassadors for our Saviour. We should be good representatives in this world for our heavenly Father.

March 16

Unknown but Used

"And Jesus, walking by the sea of Galilee, saw two brethren, Simon called Peter, and Andrew his brother, casting a net into the sea: for they were fishers" (Matt. 4:18).

"He [Andrew] *first findeth his own brother Simon, and saith unto him, We have found the Messias . . ."* (John 1:41).

Peter was well-known. His brother Andrew was not. So Andrew was referred to as Simon Peter's brother. We often experience the same thing today. Someone will say something like, "Oh, you know Tom. He's John's brother." We know right away that John is better known than Tom.

Years ago in a preacher's meeting, an older preacher who felt privileged to do what he pleased, interrupted the program to ask a preacher and his wife to sing. He said, "I want Mrs. Cavanaugh and that little man that stood up by her, I reckon it was her husband, to sing again."

Brother and Mrs. Cavanaugh went to the platform and faced the audience. It was easy to see why the old brother had been more impressed with the wife than with her husband. She was a large, attractive, well-dressed lady. He was a small, dried-up, shrimp of a man. Without a smile he said, "I am Brother Cavanaugh, and this is my wife." Then they sang. No one wants to be known because of a relationship to someone else, yet Andrew was such a man. Though he was hardly known, God used him. He brought his outstanding brother, Peter, to Christ. Often the best workers for God are people who are little known. Though they are given little recognition on earth they will enjoy rich rewards in Heaven for their faithful service.

March 17

How to Make Friends

"A man that hath friends must shew himself friendly: and there is a friend that sticketh closer than a brother" (Prov. 18:24).

We all need friends. Those in comfortable positions need friends no less than a little girl in an ill-fitting dress who is shunned by her playmates, or a little boy off by himself throwing rocks to entertain himself, because the other boys will not let him play with them.

Centuries before Dale Carnegie wrote his famous book, "How To Win Friends and Influence People," Solomon told us how to do that in the one short verse of out text.

We have to work at making friends. Talmage said, "Tell me how friendly you are, and I will tell you how friendly others are to you." An unknown writer wrote, "Smile and the world smiles with you. Weep and you weep alone." When little Mary was asked, "Why does everybody love you?" she replied, "I reckon it's because I love everybody."

Jesus is a friend that sticketh closer than a brother. We need Him as a friend most of all. When we receive Him into our hearts, He receives us. He has promised, *". . . if any man hear my voice, and open the door, I will come in to him, and will sup with him, and he with me"* (Rev. 3:20).

March 18

Busy Hands

"Whatsoever thy hand findeth to do, do it with thy might . . ." (Ecc. 9:10).
". . . establish thou the work of our hands . . ." (Psa. 90).

We should not pray for something to happen then sit in idleness waiting for God to answer. There are times when there is nothing we can do. We are shut up to faith, and we have to wait for God to act, but most of the time this is not true. There are things we can and should do.

Further, we should not wait to be given something to do. Our text tells us that our hands should find something to do. We should look for ways to serve the Lord, and we should look for ways to be a blessing to others.

Some years ago I met the daughter of Grace Livingston Hill, the great inspirational fiction writer. Mrs. Hill wrote about a hundred books in her lifetime. Her books have gone through many printings, and there is still a strong demand for them.

While I was talking with Mrs. Hill's daughter, she said, "The thing that impressed me most when I saw my mother in her casket was that her hands were not busy. That was the first time I had ever seen her hands idle." What an example from that godly woman. We too should have busy hands.

March 19

A New Way of Life

"Therefore if any man be in Christ, he is a new

*creature: old things are passed away; behold, all
things are become new"* (2 Cor. 5:17).

We are in the world, but not of the world. We are
in Christ, and that makes us new creatures. The old
interests, the old ways of thinking, and the old habits
have passed away. We have new interests, a new way
of thinking, new habits, and new pursuits. We even
have a new Father.

My friend, Dr. B. R. Lakin, now in Heaven, used
to tell the story of a woodchopper and a little prince.
The prince wandered out into the woods and heard a
woodchopper chopping down a tree. As the
woodchopper worked he was singing, "I'm a child
of the King."

The prince went to where the woodchopper was
working and interrupted him. "Why are you singing
that song?" he asked. "I'm the only child of the king."

"I'm also a child of the king," the woodchopper
answered. Then he sang:

My father is rich in houses and lands,
He holdeth the wealth of the world in His hands!
Of rubies and diamonds, of silver and gold,
His coffers are full, He has riches untold.
I once was an outcast, a stranger on earth,
A sinner by choice, and an alien by birth,
But I've been adopted, my name's written down,
An heir to a mansion, a robe, and a crown.
I'm a child of the King,
A child of the King,
With Jesus my Saviour,
I'm a child of the King.

It is wonderful to be a child of the King, and it is
a high privilege to live for Him.

March 20

Rejoice When Persecuted

"Blessed are ye, when men shall hate you . . . and shall reproach you . . . for the Son of man's sake. Rejoice ye in that day, and leap for joy: for, behold, your reward is great in heaven . . ." (Luke 6:22, 23).

No one likes to be criticized or lied about. It is discouraging when the good we do is misunderstood or misinterpreted. It is hard to bear when someone dislikes us without a reason, yet that sometimes happens.

What are we to do when others hate us and reproach us? Jesus said we are to rejoice and leap for joy. Grown-ups do not often leap for joy, but there are other ways we can let our joy be known. We certainly should not let it get us down when someone has a bad attitude. We just have to let them enjoy their misery while we enjoy our walk with the Lord.

There is further cause for us to rejoice when we are misused. Our Lord tells us that we will have a great reward in Heaven just because someone hated us and reproached us. We do not have to work for that reward. It is already in Heaven waiting for us. It will be there when we go home to be with the Lord. Those who are greatly persecuted will have a great reward. For that reason the Lord tells us to rejoice and leap for joy!

March 21

The Fruit of the Spirit

"But the fruit of the Spirit is love, joy, peace, longsuffering, gentleness, goodness, faith, Meekness, temperance: against such there is no law" (Gal. 5:22, 23).

The fruit of the Spirit belongs to those who are saved. The Bible tells us that, *"The labour of the righteous tendeth to life: the fruit of the wicked to sin"* (Prov. 10:16). On every hand we see people living in sin, and we see the results of their sins. They suffer for their deeds, and they cause others to suffer. There are laws against many of the things they do, because they bring suffering and sorrow to others. There is no law against the fruits of the Spirit, for those who bear such fruit bring encouragement and blessings to others.

The first fruit of the Spirit is love. The Spirit of God sheds abroad the love of God in our hearts (Rom. 5:5). That enables us to love as we have never loved before. We love God and the things of God, and we love family and friends with a new, deeper love. Our love reaches out to unsaved people and even to our enemies.

As we continue our walk with God, we enjoy the other fruits of the Spirit mentioned in our text. They are, joy, peace, long-suffering, gentleness, goodness, faith, meekness, and temperance. Paul tells us that if we live in the Spirit we are also supposed to walk in the Spirit (Gal. 5:25).

March 22

The Power of Stillness

". . . Their strength is to sit still" (Isa. 30:7).

In our present day world, we are conditioned to never be still. We have things to do. Things won't get done if we don't do them. We have places to go. We feel the pressure, and we drive ourselves to a frenzy.

We drink coffee and colas to pep ourselves up. Many take nerve pills to calm ourselves down, and take pain pills to stop their heads from throbbing.

God made our bodies to function without these crutches. They can be our own worst enemies physically, mentally, and spiritually.

It is calming to sit quietly by a brook and listen to the murmured passing of its water, or to sit by the sea and listen to the pounding of the surf. We cannot always sit by a stream or by the ocean, but we can make time to sit quietly, to meditate, to pray, and to let God talk to us in His still, small voice. We can put aside the rush, the agitations, and the frustrations of the day for a few minutes at least. It is surprising what a quiet time will do for our feeling, our well-being, and for our relationship with God.

March 23

Alone with God

"And the hand of the LORD was there upon me; and he said unto me, Arise, go forth into the plain, and I will there talk with thee" (Ezek. 3:22).

God's hand was upon Ezekiel. It must have been comforting for him to know that God was with him, yet he may have wondered why God was directing him to a lonely plain. There were no people there, and there would be no work there for him to do. God had promised to talk with him, and He wanted him away from people so He could get his attention.

Why must Ezekiel go to the plain? Why was Paul led to go to the desert of Arabia and stay there for three years? God talked to Ezekiel on the plain, and He talked to Paul in Arabia. On the plain God gave Ezekiel prophecies to deliver, and Paul returned from Arabia equipped for the great work God had for him to do.

There are often times when we find ourselves in

strange circumstances. Though we wonder why, we should use the time to talk with God and let Him talk to us.

March 24
Strength in Trouble

"Though I walk in the midst of trouble, thou wilt revive me . . ." (Psa. 138:7).

Trouble loves company. Often one trouble follows close upon the heels of another. Then another trouble comes, and then another, until we find ourselves walking in the midst of trouble.

In school we used to learn to bound the states. We would tell what state was on the east, what was on the north, and what was on the west and the south of a state. There are times, if we were to bound our lives as we did the states, we would have to say, "On the east I have trouble, on the north I have trials, on the west I have heartaches, and on the south I have sorrow." In short, we are walking in the midst of trouble. That is when God promises to revive us.

God does not give special blessings when they are not needed; He does give them when they are needed. When we faint beneath the load of troubles, He is present to revive us. When our load is especially heavy, we can look to God, and He will revive us.

March 25
Jesus Loves Us

"Jesus wept. Then said the Jews, Behold how he loved him!" (John 11:35, 36).

Mary and Martha, the sisters of Lazarus, had cause to doubt that Jesus loved them. They had sent word for Him to come to them when their brother was gravely ill. Jesus had received their message but had stayed where He was until after Lazarus died. When at last the sisters heard that Jesus was coming, Mary remained in the house, pouting, and Martha went out to meet Him with nagging words. She accused, *". . . Lord, if thou hadst been here, my brother had not died"* (John 11:21).

Jesus dealt with her doubts. Then she went to Mary and told her that Jesus wanted to see her. Soon Mary was weeping at Jesus feet and accusing Him with the same words Martha had used. Apparently they had said these words to each other while Jesus tarried. They were hurt, and they no longer believed that Jesus loved them.

Soon Jesus and the sisters were on their way to the tomb, and Jesus wept in such a way that even the unbelieving Jews realized that He loved Lazarus. Jesus was not weeping because Lazarus was dead, for soon He was going to bring him back to life. He was weeping with the sisters, sharing their grief. From this we learn that, even when we face of bitter disappointment or sorrow, Jesus loves us. We learn also that He shares our sorrows.

March 26

Attempt Great Things for God

"Enlarge the place of thy tent . . . lengthen thy cords, and strengthen thy stakes" (Isa. 54:2).

The prophet Isaiah challenged Israel to attempt greater things for God. They were to make their tent larger and strengthen their stakes against future storms.

We serve the same God that Israel served. Our God is not a small God. We do not need a microscope to find Him. Our God spoke in the beginning of creation, and darkness fled away. He hung the stars out to shine in space, and the angels shouted for joy. He made all things that are made, yet He is concerned with small things. He clothes the grass and feeds the birds, and He cares about us.

We need to dream greater dreams and attempt greater things for God. God has given us talents and abilities that we often do not use. He has blessings for us that we have not claimed, and He has paths of opportunity that we have not followed. We should trust Him for greater things and attempt greater things for Him.

March 27

When Your Mentor Is Gone

". . . Where is the LORD God of Elijah?. . ." (2 Kings 2:14).

Elisha left the oxen he was plowing to follow Elijah. From that hour Elijah was his mentor. Elijah remained his mentor until a chariot of fire parted them and carried him to Heaven. As Elijah went up his mantle fell from him and fluttered to the ground. Elisha picked it up and carried it with him. He returned to the Jordan, smote the water as Elijah had done, and cried, *"Where is the LORD God of Elijah?"* The power of God was upon him, and the river parted as it had for Elijah.

The sons of the prophets saw the river part and realized that the power of Elijah was upon Elisha. The home going of Elijah did not mean that God had gone away or that He no longer had a prophet. The loss of a leader does not mean that God has gone out of business.

God does not withdraw from our lives when we lose a trusted friend, a family member, or a pastor. He remains with us and is ready to bless and use us as He blessed and used the one we have lost. We can even draw closer to God after such a loss, for we must now go to Him, where once we went to the one who was our mentor. God is able and ready to be our comfort, our guide, and our mentor.

March 28

Our God Is Near

"He is near that justifieth me . . ." (Isa. 50:8).

We are taught to pray to our Father who is in Heaven (Matt. 6:9), so it is not strange that we sometimes think of God as being far away. We know that God can do anything, yet we wonder how He can hear our prayers from such a far-off place as Heaven. It is well to remember that, though God is in Heaven, He is also near. He is as near to us as the breath we breathe.

In John 14:17, Jesus said, speaking of the Holy Spirit, *". . . he dwelleth with you, and shall be in you."* In verse 20, speaking of the time after His crucifixion, resurrection, and ascension to Heaven, He continued, *"At that day ye shall know that I am in my Father, and ye in me, and I in you."* God cannot be more near than that.

It is well to remember when we pray that God is with us. He hears the whispered prayer of our hearts. When we are in trouble or in sorrow, He has promised never to leave us or forsake us. He is an ever present help in time of trouble. The old, anonymous song writer had it right when he wrote, "He promised never to leave me."

Never Alone

He promised never to leave me,
Never to leave me alone!
No, never alone, No never alone,
He promised never to leave me,
He'll claim me for His own.

March 29

Parting Is Temporary

*"But I would not have you to be ignorant, breth-
ren, concerning them which are asleep, that ye sorrow not, even as others which have no hope . . . them
also which sleep in Jesus will God bring with him"*
(1 Thess. 4:13, 14).

When we lose a loved one, it is natural to think
that the parting is permanent. If we allow that thought
to persist we sorrow as unsaved people sorrow. Paul
tells us that we are not supposed to sorrow like those
who have no hope, for we will see our saved loved
ones again.

The saved who have died are with the Lord. Paul
writes of being absent from the body and present with
the Lord (2 Cor. 5:8). When Jesus returns for the
saved, those who have died will be raised, and those
who are yet living will be caught up with them to
meet the Lord in the air (1 Thess. 4:16, 17).

The parting here is only temporary. We will see our
loved ones again. We will see them in the land where
there is no parting, and we will know them. What a
meeting that will be. There will be plenty of time, and
there will be so much to talk over and so much to

share. We are not to sorrow as one who has no hope. We are to look up and rejoice. There is coming a bright tomorrow when we will see our loved ones again.

March 30
Let Your Light Shine

"No man, when he hath lighted a candle, putteth it in a secret place, neither under a bushel, but on a candlestick, that they which come in may see the light" (Luke 11:33).

Letting a light shine is costly. A candle does not give light without burning, and we cannot let our light shine without paying a price. Sometimes the price we pay is suffering or disappointment. Our testimony is strongest when we bear our trials patiently. Trials are never easy. We prefer to have the glory without the cross. We want our light to shine without the burning, but the burning is necessary.

If we would be a lighthouse for God, we must remember that a lighthouse is placed by a churning sea, where storm-tossed waves break upon dangerous rocks. The lighthouse is not there for its own protection but for the protection of ships in danger. We are not in the world to serve ourselves. We are here to let our light shine for others.

> Others, Lord, yes others,
> Let this my motto be,
> Help me to live for others,
> That I live like Thee.

March 31
Walking Through Trial

". . . I see four men loose, walking in the midst of

the fire, and they have no hurt; and the form of the fourth is like the Son of God" (Dan. 3:25).

Three men, Shadrach, Meshach, and Abednego, were bound and cast into a fiery furnace because they refused to worship the golden image King Nebuchadnezzar had made. They believed God would deliver them, but they told the king that whether God delivered them or not, they would not worship his god.

These men vowed to be faithful to God regardless of the consequences. That did not keep them out of the fire, but it did free them of their bonds. Further, they did not have to go through the fire alone. One like the Son of God walked with them, and that enabled them to walk in the fire without being burned.

We all have to walk through fiery trials. To paraphrase the words of an old songwriter, God has not promised to carry us to the sky on flowery beds of ease. We must climb to reach the mountaintop. We must battle storms to grow strong, and we must pass through fire to be refined. We should be faithful to God no matter what the cost. When we are faithful, we will not have to walk alone, and our faith will be a testimony to others.

Devotions for April

April 1

The Singing of the Birds

"The flowers appear on the earth; the time of the singing of birds is come..." (Song of Solomon 2:12).

Birds sing at different times. Some sing in the early morning. Others sing through the day, and some sing at night. The robin sings its last song at the end of the day, and the nightingale sings in the night.

Birds are carefree creatures. They go about their tasks of nest-building, hatching, and caring for their young with song. They do not worry about what they will eat, for God provides for them. Jesus used birds as an example of God's care and ended by saying that we are of more value than they are (Matt. 6:26).

The singing of birds announces that springtime has arrived. After a winter of cold and snow and sleet, the sun will shine again, and the flowers will bud and blossom.

When winter comes in our lives and we go through days so dark we wonder if the sun will ever shine again, we should listen for the singing of birds and watch for the flowers to bloom.

April 2

Light Not Seen

"And now men see not the bright light which is in the clouds..." (Job. 37:21).

When things go wrong it is not easy to look on the bright side. That is when we need wings of faith so we can soar above the storms that whirls about us.

When I used to fly a small Piper Cub plane, one winter day when I had to fly under a dark cloud cover. Not a ray of sunlight pierced the clouds, and the ground beneath me was in shadows. Then I came to a place where there was an opening in the clouds, and I could see blue sky above them. I decided to climb up through the opening and see what the clouds looked like from the topside.

I was not prepared for the beauty I saw when I was above the clouds. The sky above me was cloudless, and the sun was shining in all its radiance. The clouds beneath me were silver white, and they looked like a billowy ocean stretching away in all directions. I was seeing the light in the clouds, where before I had seen only darkness. Thank God there is light even when we do not see it.

April 3
What God Uses

". . . and Moses took the rod of God in his hand" (Ex. 4:20).

For forty years Moses had been a sheepherder in Midian. Now he is returning to Egypt to stand before powerful King Pharaoh as God's representative. His only credential was a shepherd's staff that he had cut somewhere in the desert, but that staff had now become the *"rod of God."* With it Moses would perform miracles and bring the proud king to his knees.

Moses was reluctant to return to Egypt. He had failed there years before when he attempted to assist his people, and he was sure that he would fail again if he returned. But that did not take into account the *"rod of God."* God promised Moses that He would be with him, and He demonstrated to him that He would use his simple shepherd's staff to accomplish His purpose. As long as Moses controlled the staff it was only good for herding sheep, but when God controlled it wondrous things happened.

God does not ask us to accomplish things for Him in our own power. Nor does He ask us to use that which we do not possess. He only asks that we be willing to serve Him in the way of His choosing. He will use whatever talents we have, and He will give us guidance and the ability to do the work of His choosing. Moses did not accomplish anything until he was willing to do God's bidding.

April 4
Help When Tempted

"For in that he himself hath suffered being tempted, he is able to succour them that are tempted" (Heb. 2:18).

A young lady who had recently been saved was dismayed that she was still being tempted to sin. She had thought that with salvation came deliverance from temptation. The Lord has not promised that we will not be tempted. Instead, He has promised to give us victory over temptation.

Even Jesus was tempted. The Bible tells us that He was tempted at all points like as we are, but He did not sin (Heb. 4:15). Satan dared to tempt Jesus, so he will surely tempt us. We are not strong enough to overcome his temptations, but Jesus is.

There is a most interesting word in our text. It is the word, *"succour."* Succour is a word that we almost never use, but there is no other word that has the same meaning. It means to run to the aid of one who is in trouble. That means that Jesus will run to our aid when we are tempted. When temptation is too much for you, run to meet Him and let Him give you victory over temptation.

April 5
The Stairway to Victory

"By whom (Jesus) *also we have access by faith into this grace wherein we stand, and rejoice in hope of the glory of God. . . . we glory in tribulations also: knowing that tribulation worketh patience"* (Rom. 5:2, 3).

Strange phrasing! Words in contrast! How can we rejoice in hope and glory in tribulation? Rejoicing in hope we understand. Glorying in tribulation is more difficult. Paul continues in verses four and five to show that tribulation is a stairway to victory.

Tribulation builds patience. The next step is experience. We learn from our trials, and our faith grows stronger. The next step is the hope of future glory. We are not ashamed of this hope, because it leads to the next step. The Holy Spirit fills our heart with the love of God, and that gives us maturity. We love God, and we love our fellowman. Loving others leads to a right relationship with others. We do not do unkind things to those we love (Rom. 13:10). We do to them as we expect them to do to us.

April 6
The Sure Foundation

"He brought me up also out of an horrible pit, out of the miry clay, and set my feet upon a rock, and established my goings" (Psa. 40:2).

So much in life is uncertain, we need something

we can depend on. The life of the Psalmist's was no different than our lives today. He saw himself in a horrible pit, needing deliverance. Beyond the pit was miry clay. It seemed there was no place to set his feet, so he waited patiently for the Lord (verse 1). He called upon the Lord, and the Lord heard his prayer. The Lord lifted him from the pit and set his feet upon a rock. The rock was a sure foundation. God even put a new song in his mouth (verse 3).

Notice what the Psalmist did and what the Lord did. The Psalmist could only recognize his condition, call upon the Lord, and wait for Him to answer his prayer. The Lord heard his cry, lifted him from the pit, delivered him from the miry clay, and established his goings. That means that the Lord gave him strength to live victoriously.

We cannot deliver ourselves from sin and its consequences, but our Lord is able to deliver us. We can follow the same path the Psalmist followed, and we can find the deliverance and the victory that he found. Like him, we should call upon the Lord, and wait patiently for Him to answer.

April 7

Comforting Arms

"The eternal God is thy refuge, and underneath are the everlasting arms" (Deut. 33:27).

Nothing can be more comforting to a hurt child than a mother's arms. Big people get hurt also, but they are too grown-up and to self-reliant to run to a mother's arms, so what are they to do?

Unsaved people can only suffer through their pain with such poor comfort as their friends and family can give them. The refuge they need can only be found in God. Jesus will save them if they will trust in Him, and He will become their comforter. We who are saved have a refuge in the everlasting arms of our heavenly Father. He is there for us to trust. He has promised to never leave us or forsake us. Jesus promised to give us a comforter to abide with us forever (John 14:16). Our comforter is the Holy Spirit. As a troubled child runs to the arms of a mother, we can run to the arms of our heavenly Father.

April 8

God's Call to Service

"... *Whom shall I send, and who will go for us? Then said I, Here am I; send me*" (Isa. 6:8).

The call to serve God is not just for preachers and other full-time Christian workers. We are all called to serve God in one way or another. God knows our talents and where we can best serve. We need to find His will and serve in the way of His choosing.

Isaiah received his call in a time of national mourning. King Uzziah had died and in the time of mourning, Isaiah had a vision of God in all His glory and received his call. God often comes to us in a special way in times of sorrow, sickness, or trial.

As a result of his vision of God, Isaiah saw himself as a man of unclean lips, and he realized that others were in the same condition. It was then that he received his call and answered, *"Here am I; send me."* God will send anyone who is willing to go. He still is asking, *"Whom shall I send, and who will go for us?"* God help us to answer as Isaiah did, *"Here am I; send me."*

April 9

The Source of Our Righteousness

". . . their righteousness is of me, saith the LORD" (Isa. 54:17).

We can never make ourselves good enough to be saved. We cannot atone for our sins. Therefore we can never attain the holiness that God demands. God gives us salvation as a free gift, and He imputes His righteousness to us. *"For by grace are ye saved through faith; and that not of yourselves: it is the gift of God: Not of works, lest any man should boast"* (Eph. 2:8-9). God does the saving, so we do not have to worry about saving ourselves. God's gift of salvation does not mean that we are not to live for Him. We are to rejoice in our salvation, draw near to God, and live for Him because we love Him.

God is our heavenly Father, and we can go to Him in prayer as a child goes to an earthly father. We need not feel unworthy, for God has given His righteousness to us. Jesus had no sin of His own, but He bore our sins on the cross. That means that we appear before God as if we had never sinned. Our righteousness is of the Lord. Thank Him, praise Him, and serve Him.

April 10

Jesus Is Our Shepherd

"He shall feed his flock like a shepherd: he shall gather the lambs with his arm, and carry them in his bosom . . ." (Isa. 40:11).

A mother often carries a small baby in her bosom. When the child is older and has learned to walk, its short legs still cannot keep pace with her, so it often holds up its arms and cries, "Mama, carry me." When we find the pathway too rough for us to navigate alone, we too can ask the heavenly Father to carry us. If we allow pride to keep us from asking for our Father's aid, we have to tread the difficult path alone. That should not be, for the Heavenly Father wants to carry us in His loving arms.

In Luke 15, the good shepherd goes after the lost sheep until He finds it. Then He carries it back to the fold. In Psalm 23, the shepherd leads his sheep, feeds his sheep, and protects his sheep. Our good shepherd is Jesus. He wants to care for us, and, when the road of life is rough, He wants to carry us in His loving arms. He wants us to call upon Him when we need His help.

April 11
Wait Upon the Lord

"Wait on the LORD: be of good courage, and he shall strengthen thine heart: wait, I say, on the LORD" (Psa. 27:14).

It is not easy to wait on the Lord. We are impatient. We want things to happen now, but God moves with measured tread. He has all eternity, and He knows the end from the beginning. So He does things in the time and in the way that is best for us. We should be patient and wait upon the Lord.

Waiting on the Lord teaches us faith, dependence, and patience. If we could get everything we want when we want it, we would be like spoiled children. So God measures to us what is best for us in the time that is right for us. When we are discouraged and ready to give up, God will be present to strengthen us.

Even when things look bad, we should be of good

courage. The Bible is filled with examples of God answering prayer and carrying His children in troubled times. He is the same God today, and He is ready to come to our aid when we need Him.

April 12

Never Give Up

"I had fainted, unless I had believed to see the goodness of the LORD in the land of the living" (Psa. 27:13).

The Psalmist is writing of failing in the spiritual sense, but he did not faint. He had the Lord to support him, and he believed in the goodness of the Lord in the land of the living. To faint is to fall unless another supports us. That means that he believed God would bless him and meet his needs.

We know that God will bless us in Heaven, but it is not easy to believe in the goodness of God when we are facing tough times on earth. When we have failed and are ready to give up, we must pause, be still, and believe in the goodness of God.

God loves us. He knows when we face difficulties, and He is able to meet our need. The key word in our text is *"believe."* We must believe in the goodness of God and in His desire to care for us. We need not faint. We can believe in God and know that He will sustain us.

April 13

Testing For Our Good

". . . we went through fire and through water: but thou broughtest us out into a wealthy place" (Psa. 66:12).

Testing is never easy. Sometimes the testing is so

severe we feel that we cannot go on. We may think that we will be overwhelmed if we try. We can even come to a place where we feel there is nothing left for us but failure. When that happens we should walk by faith, not by feelings. We should look to our God, not at the conditions around us.

Faith often falters when we feel the heat of the fire, or when floods of water threaten us. When trials come we need our faith to be strong. We need to realize that the trials may only be a time of testing that is for our good.

We do not gain strength when we are at ease. It is struggle and trial that toughens us. The captain of a ship is stronger, more confident, wiser, and more capable after he has gone through some storms. We too are stronger after we have piloted our ship of life through some storms and God has turned the testing to our advantage.

April 14

Shelter and Protection

"O Jerusalem, Jerusalem, . . . how often would I have gathered thy children together, even as a hen gathereth her chickens under her wings, and ye would not!" (Matt. 23:37).

Jesus uttered these words with a heavy heart. He had come to His own people, and they had not received Him. Our text was spoken to the Jews, but it can help us understand something of the love and compassion that Jesus has. He wants both to shelter and protect His people.

As a boy growing up on the farm, I often saw a mother hen gather her chickens under her wings. Mama often tied a mother hen so she wouldn't wander off, and her chickens forged around her. If a sudden, spring rain came, the hen would spread her wings and call her chickens, and they would run under her for shelter. In fair weather, if a hawk or a crow flew over, the mother hen knew they posed a danger to her chickens, and she would call them to shelter from danger beneath her wings.

Jesus had seen mother hens shelter and protect their chickens as I had when I was a boy. He knew His hearers had seen the same thing. He was telling them that He could not shelter and protect them because they had refused to come to Him. The same principle works today. We must come to Jesus if we are to have His protections and His blessings.

April 15

God Works in the Night

". . . and the LORD caused the sea to go back by a strong east wind all that night . . ." (Ex. 14:21).

The Israelites were fleeing from Egypt, and Pharaoh's army was pursuing them. When they reached the sea there was no way to cross, and they were hemmed in by the wilderness. In the face of what seemed a hopeless position, Moses told the people not to fear. *"And Moses said unto the people, Fear ye not, stand still, and see the salvation of the LORD . . ."* (verse 13).

The rest of the day passed, and night came with no evidence that God was doing anything for them. What a long, frightening night that must have been. They could hear the tossing waves of the sea in front of them, and they knew that Pharaoh's army was behind them and would overtake them in the morning. To make matters worse, a terrible east wind battered their camp all night.

They must have thought that God had forgotten

them, but God worked for them all that night. The next morning they did see the salvation of the Lord. He had parted the sea so they could cross safely. There are times when we see no evidence that God is answering our prayers. We think that things are out of control, but God has not lost control. God is working for us whether we see the evidence of His work or not. In due time we will see that He has answered our prayers in the way that is best for us.

April 16
Pray Always
"Watch ye therefore, and pray always . . ." (Luke 21:36).

There are many reasons why we should pray always, but that is not easy to do. Tired after a day at work, we can easily cut our prayer time short and fall into bed, or we can miss it altogether. In the morning, with the pressures of the new day upon us, it is easy to skip our time of prayer, eat a hurried breakfast, dress, and rush off to work without realizing that we are ill prepared for the day.

We need time alone with God to give us strength to face what the day may bring. So, what are we to do when the pressures of the day have cheated us out of our time alone with God? We can pray aloud on our way to work if we are in the car alone. If there are others in the car, we can pray silently. After we arrive in the workplace, we can stay in touch with God in whispered prayers, and at lunchtime we may be able to slip away from others for a few quiet moments of prayer.

This kind of praying cannot take the place of our regular times of prayer, but like snacks, taken between meals, it is better than no praying at all.

April 17

Help in Prayer

". . . but the Spirit itself maketh intercession for us" (Rom. 8:26).

". . . who (Christ) *also maketh intercession for us"* (Rom. 8:34).

When a praying mother dies one is apt to ask, "I wonder who will pray for me now?" On such an occasion we need not feel that we are left without prayer support, for we have the promise that both Jesus and the Holy Spirit will intercede for us. We do not know how to pray as we should, so the Holy Spirit acts as our interpreter. We may groan within ourselves, not fully understanding our needs, but we can rest assured that the intercessions of the Holy Spirit will be the correct petitions.

The Holy Spirit is not the only One who prays for us. The Lord Jesus Christ makes intercessions for us at the right hand of the Father. We need not fear that our prayers have not been heard, and there is no question that they will be understood. If we do not see the answer to our prayer at once, that does not mean that God has not heard. We must believe that the answer is on the way and wait upon the Lord.

April 18

God Works for Our Good

"And we know that all things work together for good to them that love God . . ." (Rom. 8:28).

When everything seems to be going wrong, we who love God can rest upon this promise. This calls for some heart examination. Do we really love God, and are we serving Him because we love Him? Three times Jesus asked Peter if he loved Him. Jesus knew that Peter loved him, but He wanted Peter to know that He loved him. Just as Peter did, we need to know that we love God.

The promise in our text is not in the past tense or in the future tense. It does not mean that things have worked for our good in the past, or that things are going to work for our good in the future. Doubtless things have worked for our good in the past, and they will work for our good in the future, but the point is that they are working for our good right now. This is true even when we do not see any evidence that things are working for our good. Even when we do not see what we expected, we need to continue to believe that God is working for us.

Further, it is not one thing that is working for our good; it is all things working together for our good. Things are not working one against another, but in harmony with each other. As the various sounds of a great orchestra work together to make beautiful music, God will take the various things in our lives and make harmony with them. As the various colors of paint in an artist's palette work together to make a beautiful painting, the things we are going through can make our lives beautiful.

April 19

Sufficient Grace

". . . My grace is sufficient for thee: for my strength is made perfect in weakness. Most gladly therefore will I rather glory in my infirmities, that the power of Christ may rest upon me" (2 Cor. 12:9).

On this occasion the great Apostle Paul did not get his prayer answered in the way he had requested. Three times he had prayed for a thorn in his flesh to be removed, but God did not remove it. Instead God told him that His grace was sufficient. God's grace is favor, loving kindness, and mercy. That was all Paul needed. The weakness caused by his affliction made him more dependent upon God's power, and that made him more effective and gave God greater glory.

God does not always answer our prayers in the way we want them answered, but that does not mean that He has not heard our prayer. God always hears the prayer of faith, but, in His wisdom and foreknowledge, He sometimes answers in a way that is different from what we requested. We do not know how to pray as we should, and sometimes we request things that would not be good for us. In faith we should accept the answer God gives as His will for our lives.

April 20
The Glory of God

"The heavens declare the glory of God; the firmament sheweth his handywork" (Psa. 19:1).

Paul tells us that we can know that God is the creator by the things that are made (Rom. 1:20). Our text says, *"The heavens declare the glory of God."*

The following poem covers this subject in a wonderful way.

The Power of God
Has anyone measured the water
Contained in the oceans and seas?
Has anyone found the machinery
That creates the wind and the breeze?

Has anyone weighed the mountains
Or measured the rocks piled high?
Has anyone found the magnet
That holds the stars in the sky?

Has anyone found the lantern
Behind the lightnings flash,
Or found the huge bass drummer
That causes the thunder's crash?

Has anyone ever counted
Grains of sand on the shore,
Or found the molds for the seashells
Washed with the tide's loud roar?

Has anyone made the tiny seeds
Burst open and grow in the sod?
I wonder if we can really know
How great and powerful is God!
                                —Nellie Thompson

April 21

God Gives Victory

"Behold, God is my salvation; I will trust, and not be afraid: for the LORD JEHOVAH is my strength and my song . . ." (Isa. 12:2).

Wonderful promises! It is wonderful when we can say, *"God is my salvation . . . JEHOVAH is my strength."* God is all powerful. He created the universe for His own pleasure (Rev. 4:11). As Jehovah, the mighty God, relates to man, He saves us. Jehovah gives us strength. I can trust and not be afraid, and that puts a song in my heart.

There are Christians who do not have the song mented in our text. They plod along day after day, knowing that they are going to Heaven but not enjoying the journey.

Years ago old-time Methodists talked about joy bells ringing in their hearts. In a testimony meeting they would talk about losing their joy because they had sinned. Then they would speak of confessing their sin and of the joy bells returning and ringing in their hearts again.

Our victory is in God. He saves us, and He gives us strength. We can trust in Him and rejoice in Him.

April 22
Overflowing Wells of Water

"Therefore with joy shall ye draw water out of the wells of salvation" (Isa. 12:3).

This verse harks back to the preceding verse. There we are told that God is our salvation and that Jehovah is our strength. Because of that I can draw water from the wells of salvation.

Jesus told the woman of Samaria that if she would drink of the water that He would give, she would never thirst again (John 4:14). While Jesus was on the cross, He cried, *"I thirst."* He bore our sins, and He bore our thirst. Now all who thirst can come to Him and drink.

Jesus spoke of the well of salvation, but there are other wells. There is a well of victory for those who feel defeated. There is a well of peace for those who are in turmoil. There is a well of contentment for those who can find no rest. There is a well of assurance for those who are uncertain. There is a well of joy for those who are sad in heart, and there are many other wells from which to drink.

April 23
Give Thanks Unto the Lord

"Give thanks unto the LORD, call upon his name, make known his deeds among the people" (1 Chr. 16:8).

We should come into God's presence with thanksgiving. Expressing our gratitude prepares our hearts for prayer, and praying enables us to be blessed and to share God's blessings with others. God uses people who pray.

The great evangelist, Billy Sunday, is a good example. Harry D. Clarke, who was his song leader for a number of years, bore witness of his prayer life. After Billy Sunday had gone to his reward, Harry became my song leader. One day while he was working with me he told me how Billy Sunday used to pray. He said he would hear him talking in his hotel room and think he had a guest. Then he would discover that Mr. Sunday was talking to the Lord.

Mr. Sunday had a habit of talking to the Lord while he was shaving or dressing. He would pray something like the following: "Now, Lord, You know I will soon be going to the tabernacle to preach. There will be a great crowd there, and I have to have Your help if I'm going to reach them."

Mr. Sunday said that he never preached without asking the Lord to bless the service, and he never failed to thank Him when He did. Like Mr. Sunday, we should stay in touch with the Lord, and we should never fail to thank Him for His blessings.

April 24

Showing Gratitude

"IT is a good thing to give thanks unto the LORD, and to sing praises unto thy name, O most High: To shew forth thy lovingkindness in the morning, and thy faithfulness every night" (Psa. 92:1, 2).

Words of gratitude are easily spoken. It is also easy to forget to say them. We should thank the Lord for all

His blessings, and we should go beyond simple words of thanksgiving and sing praises to His name.

It is good to begin our day with praise and worship. That will bring joy to our hearts, and it will help us to be a testimony to others. To *"show forth"* God's lovingkindness is a way of witnessing. Even when people turn away, they cannot fail to see the joy and victory in our lives. We must not allow the devil to take away our victory. All day long we should be a testimony for our Lord.

God shows His lovingkindness in the morning and His faithfulness every night. We should start our day and end our day with thankfulness and praise.

April 25
Help in Time of Need

"But I am poor and needy; yet the Lord thinketh upon me: thou art my help and my deliverer; make no tarrying, O my God" (Psa. 40:17).

The Psalmist must have marveled that God had him in mind in spite of his weakness and need. He realized that God was his helper and deliverer, and that gave him courage to demand that God come to his aid without delay.

Most of us have times when our spirits are low. We feel that nothing we have is satisfying and that we have needs that cannot be met from any earthly source. In such times we can indulge in self-pity, or we can remember that God cares for us and call upon Him.

There are times when we have no earthly help, and we have to turn to God. At such times we should be thankful for the privilege of prayer. Prayer is a lifeline that lays hold upon the promises of God. Sometimes God answers our prayers at once. Other times, for reasons unknown to us, the answer is delayed. When that happens, we must hold on by faith, knowing that God will answer in a time and in the way that is best for us.

April 26

Unseen Help

"Are they not all ministering spirits (angels), *sent forth to minister for them who shall be heirs of salvation?"* (Heb. 1:14).

Angels are created spirit-beings. They are higher in the scale of creation than man, but lower than Jesus. They are created sons of God. They are invisible spirits unless they choose to make themselves visible, and they are anonymous. The Bible gives only the names of two of God's angels, Michael and Gabriel.

Angels have greater strength and wisdom than men, so they are able to do for us what no man can do. When we are thanking God for His blessings, let us not forget to thank Him for the angels He has sent to minister to us.

April 27

How to Know the Will of God

". . . as the servants of Christ, doing the will of God from the heart" (Eph. 6:6).

True Christians want to live in the will of God. Like Jesus, they often pray, *". . . not my will, but thine, be done" (Luke 22:42).* Yet, they often have difficulty knowing what God would have them to do. Following, I list some ways to determine the will of God and some safeguards that will keep us from making mistakes.

First, anything we feel impressed to do should be

considered in the light of God's Word. God never leads us to do anything that is contrary to the plain teachings of His Word.

Not every decision we have to make is covered in the Bible, so there are times when we have to depend upon the leading of the Holy Spirit. Sometimes the Holy Spirit leads by an impression upon the heart. Often it is difficult to tell the difference in our own desires and the leading of the Spirit. When that happens it is wise to pray and to wait. Our own desires usually fade away with time, but the leading of the Spirit grows stronger. His leading can become so strong that there is no longer any doubt regarding God's will.

Another way to determine God's will is by open and closed doors. There are times when more than one door is open to us, and we do not know which way to turn. Usually, if we wait and pray we will come to know that some of the open doors are not God's will for us. In time, some doors will close. Others may open, adding to the confusion, but caution, waiting, and praying will help to determine how God is leading.

April 28

Learn Not to Worry

". . . fret not thyself in any wise to do evil" (Psa. 37:8).

My version of this verse is, "Don't get upset and do something that is wrong." Things do not always go the way we want them to, and it's human to worry when they don't.

It is well to remember that worry doesn't solve

any problems. It can only makes matters worse. An unknown writer gave a needed message in the following poem.

The Robin and the Sparrow

Said the robin to the sparrow,
"I would really like to know
Why these anxious human beings
Rush about and worry so."

Said the sparrow to the robin,
"Friend, I think that it must be
That they have no Heavenly Father,
Such as cares for you and me."

Whatever problems we have today, we should put them in the hands of our heavenly Father. He never worries, and He knows how to solve our problems. We must have patience and wait upon Him to lead us to the solutions we need.

April 29

The City of God

"Glorious things are spoken of thee, O city of God. Selah" (Psa. 87:3).
"But now they desire a better country, that is, an heavenly . . . for he hath prepared for them a city" (Heb. 11:16).

God has prepared a city for the redeemed. That city is the crown jewel of Heaven. It is a beautiful city, and it is located in a better country. There are streams in that country. In Psalm 46:4 we read, *"There is a river, the streams whereof shall make glad the city of God."* John wrote, *"AND he shewed me a pure river of water of life . . . "* (Rev. 22:1). Trees of life grows on both sides of the river. There must be many trees in that better country.

It is comforting to know that one day we will go to that heavenly city in that better country. In that heavenly country we will be in perfect health, and we will be young forever. We will be with loved ones who have gone on before us, and we will know as we are known.

Heaven will be an active place. We will have plenty of energy, and we will never grow tired. We will not even need to sleep, for there will be no night there. We will worship and praise God, and we will visit with loved ones, with angels, with prophets, and with apostles.

April 30
Fullness of Joy

"And these things write we unto you, that your joy may be full" (1 John 1:4).

Being saved should bring gladness, not sadness. True Christianity is not expressed with a long face and a sanctimonious voice. The true Christian can and should spread sunshine.

The great preacher, Talmage, said: "If religion is going to put the piano out of tune, and clog the feet of my children running through the hall, and sour the bread, and put crape on the doorbell, I do not want it to come into my house. I paid six dollars to hear Jenny Lynn warble. I never paid a cent to hear anybody groan."

A sour face and a bad disposition will not make friends or draw people to Christ. Trusting in the Lord and walking in fellowship with Him will bring joy to the heart, put a smile on the lips, and give one a cheerful disposition.

Devotions for May

May 1
The Power of God's Word

"Through faith we understand that the worlds were framed by the word of God, so that things which are seen were not made of things which do appear" (Heb. 11:3).

The things we see were made of things we cannot see. There was a time when there was nothing to see. Then God spoke and there was a universe to see.

It takes breath to speak, and breath takes energy. That means that God used energy to create. Job said, *"The spirit of God hath made me, and the breath of the Almighty hath given me life"* (Job 33:4).

The vastness of the universe is staggering. In our galaxy alone there are an estimated four billion stars with their accompanying planets and moons. In the entire universe, spreading through space for millions of light-years, it is estimated that there are fifty billion billion stars. The greatness of our God is beyond comprehension. We should worship in wonder and praise Him every day of our lives.

May 2
Our God Is Worthy

"Thou art worthy, O Lord, to receive glory and honour and power: for thou hast created all things,

and for thy pleasure they are and were created" (Rev. 4:11).

In the 4th chapter of The Revelation, John saw 24 elders seated on thrones. They were wearing white robes and crowns of gold. These elders represent a blood-washed, royal priesthood. Only the church fulfills that description.

John saw the elders fall down to worship before the throne of God. That tells us that we will worship God in Heaven. We need to get in the habit of worshiping God while we are yet in the world. Then we will be ready to worship Him in eternity. In Psalm 29:2 we are told, *"Give unto the LORD the glory due unto his name; worship the LORD in the beauty of holiness."*

We should make every day a day of worship and praise. Our very lives should honor and praise God. Living for the glory of God will make us happy and make a blessing to others.

May 3

It Pays to Wait upon the Lord

"But they that wait upon the LORD shall renew their strength; they shall mount up with wings as eagles; they shall run, and not be weary; and they shall walk, and not faint" (Isa. 40:31).

In this busy, rushing world it is not easy to wait. We grow impatient when we have to wait for any reason. The Bible tells us to wait upon the Lord, but we find that hard to do. We grow impatient when God does not answer our prayers right away.

It is not right to be impatient with others. It is

much worse not to have patience with God. When we are impatient, God may send trials to teach us patience. In James 1:3 we read, *"Knowing this, that the trying of your faith worketh patience."* Then in verse 4 we are told to *"But let patience have her perfect work, that ye may be perfect and entire, wanting nothing."* One of life's great lessons is to learn patience.

Our text for today promises great things to those who wait upon the Lord. Let us read it again. *"But they that wait upon the LORD shall renew their strength; they shall mount up with wings as eagles; they shall run, and not be weary; and they shall walk, and not faint."*

For our own good and for the good of others, we should learn patience and learn to wait upon the Lord.

May 4

Wait upon the Lord

"But I am poor and needy: make haste unto me, O God . . ." (Psa. 70:5).

King David must have really been discouraged when he wrote the text we are using today. His prayer is almost humorous. Can you imagine a king being poor and needy?

David was chosen by God to be King of Israel. He became a great king. He had many friends He had great musical talent. He was one of the great hymn writers of all time. Yet, he cries, *". . . I am poor and needy . . ."*, and he asks God to make haste and come to him. Can you imagine God being tardy, yet David prays for God to hurry. God is never late, so He does not have to hurry.

Sometimes we feel that God is far from us. When we pray and our prayer is not answered at once we wonder why. We may even feel sorry for ourselves and cry as David did.

There are days when we all feel discouraged. When that happens we should not wallow in self-pity. We should trust and pray and wait upon the Lord.

When God does not answer our prayers at once, it may be that He is trying to teach us something— like patience, maybe.

May 5
Never Lonely

"The LORD is my shepherd; I shall not want" (Psa. 23:1).

David realized that he belonged to the Shepherd and the Shepherd belonged to him. This was a close relationship, for the Shepherd led him, fed him, protected him, and promised to be with him, even in the shadow of death.

We can claim the same promises that David claimed. The Lord is also our Shepherd. He has promised, *". . . I will never leave thee, nor forsake thee"* (Heb. 13:5).

Far back in the country a preacher saw an old, old lady seated in a rocker on the front porch of her cabin.

"Are you all alone, auntie?" he asked.

"Just me and Jesus," she responded.

She was alone, but she was not lonely. Those who know the Lord need never be lonely. He is our Shepherd, and we are His sheep. Our Shepherd cares for His sheep. He leads them beside still waters. He makes them to lie down in green pastures. He protects them from evil. He is with them when death threatens, and He promises that goodness and mercy will follow them.

May 6
A Light in Darkness

"Thy word is a lamp unto my feet, and a light unto my path" (Psa. 119:105).

The Lord knows that sometimes we walk in spiritual darkness, so He has given us His Word for a light. Other lights often fail us, but the Word of God never fails us. His Word is a lamp for our feet so we can see where we are stepping, and His Word is a light on our pathway so we can see where we are going.

A light is of no help if we do not turn it on, and the Word of God will not help us if we do not read it. Thank God that His Word is available, and we can turn to it when our way is obscured by darkness.

Not only can we use the light, we can share the light with others. All around us are people who are walking in darkness. It may be the darkness of sorrow. Or it may be the darkness of trouble or suffering. It can even be the darkness of fear. Whatever the cause of the darkness, we can share the light of God's Word with them.

May 7
Secure in God's Love

"For I am persuaded, that neither death, nor life, nor angels, nor principalities, nor powers, nor things present, nor things to come, Nor height, nor depth, nor any other creature, shall be able to separate us from the love of God, which is in Christ Jesus our

Lord" *(*Rom. 8:38, 39).

Paul calls the roll of everything we can imagine that might come between us and God. That roll includes death, life, angels, principalities, powers, things present, things to come, height, and depth. Then for fear he had missed something, he adds, *". . . nor any other creature, shall be able to separate us from the love of God, which is in Christ Jesus our Lord."*

Paul covers every dimension to assure us that we are secure in God's love. The way God had delivered him from trial after trial had led him to his victorious persuasion. He had found God's love dependable in all kinds of circumstances, and he assures us that we are also safe in His love.

May 8

How to Worship God

"God is a Spirit: and they that worship him must worship him in spirit and in truth" (John 4:24).

The woman at the well was concerned about where to worship God. In this verse Jesus told her that the question was not where to worship God but how to worship Him.

God is a spiritual being. We cannot see Him, hear Him, or touch Him, but we can perceive His presence. We are spiritual beings, and we have spiritual perception. We can sense the presence of God. By meditation and prayer we can worship God in spirit, but Jesus said that we must also worship Him in truth as well. We must come to Him in faith, knowing that He is the rewarder of those who diligently seek Him. And we are to come to Him with honest, sincere hearts if we are to worship Him in truth.

May 9

The Lord Is Our Help

"My help cometh from the LORD, which made heaven and earth. He will not suffer thy foot to be moved: he that keepth thee will not slumber" (Psa. 121:2, 3).

In this verse we are reminded that our help comes from the Lord who created the universe. He has power beyond the power of all others, yet He is concerned with the small things in our lives, even with where we place our feet.

Here is blessed assurance. The One who never sleeps watches over us while we sleep. I am only one of the billions of people on earth, but God knows me and cares for me. I am His child, and He is my loving Father. Though God has charge of a universe too vast to imagine, He still cares for me, and He is concerned about the affairs of my life. He knows my trials, my weaknesses, and my fears. When Satan tries me beyond my strength, God is my keeper, and my help comes from Him.

May 10

Footsteps That Bless

"The steps of a good man are ordered by the LORD: and he delighteth in his way. Though he fall, he shall not be utterly cast down: for the LORD upholdeth him with his hand" (Psa. 37:23, 24).

Footsteps come from somewhere; and they lead somewhere. They leave a trail for others to follow. Footsteps can lead others in the right direction or they can lead them astray. Footsteps leave tracks that may remain long after the one who made them has gone. How symbolic of one's testimony. The influence of a life can affect present and future generations. We should always make sure that our footsteps are going in the right direction.

It is good to know that our steps are ordered by the Lord, that even if we fall, He will uphold us with His mighty hand. Let us delight in the will of the Lord and let us rejoice that He is directing our footsteps.

May 11

Christ the Song

"The LORD is my strength and song, and is become my salvation" (Psa. 118:14).

More songs have been written about Jesus than about any other person who ever lived. How dark this world would be if there were no songs about Jesus. What a blessing it is that He has given us songs to cheer us when we face trials or walk through darkness. In Psalm 40:3, David wrote, *"And he hath put a new song in my mouth, even praise unto our God: many shall see it, and fear, and shall trust in the LORD."*

Praising God in song has ever been a large part of worship. Nothing can so gladden the heart as praising Him. One of the glories of Heaven will be songs of praise.

It is well that we get in the habit of praising and worshiping God while we are yet in this world so that we will not feel out of place when we reach the land of glory and praise.

May 12

The Meaning of Faith

"NOW faith is the substance of things hoped for, the evidence of things not seen" (Heb. 11:1).

Hebrews 11 is the faith chapter of the Bible. The word faith is used in this chapter 25 times. The chapter tells us what faith is, then it calls the roll of Bible characters who walked by faith. The chapter ends by telling us that without Christians in future generations the record would not be perfect or complete. That means that we can walk by faith today.

We cannot be saved without faith, and we cannot live victorious lives without faith. By faith we receive Jesus as Saviour. By faith we face our trials. By faith we find comfort in times of sorrow. By faith we overcome temptation. By faith we can climb our own Jacob's ladder of prayer to the throne room and lay our petitions at Jesus' feet.

By faith we can have victory in life, and when our time comes for us to leave this world, we can have a victorious crossing to Immanuel's Land.

May 13

A Joyful Testimony

"These things have I spoken unto you, that my joy might remain in you, and that your joy might be full" (John 15:11).

"A merry heart doeth good like a medicine: but a broken spirit drieth the bones" (Prov. 17:22).

Jesus wants His joy to be in us, and He wants our joy to be full. Christians who have no joy have poor testimonies. Nobody wants to be like a whining, whimpering, complaining Christian. They are like a cold wind on a rainy day. They carry a depressing atmosphere with them, and when they enter a room their presence is depressing.

Joyful Christians brighten a room when they enter, and they lift the spirits of those about them. It is delightful to be in their presence. Their confident assurance makes others want to be like them.

We must walk close to Jesus to have the fullness of His joy. If we drift from His presence or go into sin we lose our joy. When we confess our coldness or our sin, He restores our joy, and, with the fullness of His joy, we can win others to him. After David had sinned, he prayed,

"Restore unto me the joy of thy salvation . . . Then will I teach transgressors thy ways; and sinners shall be converted unto thee" (Psa. 51:12, 13).

May 14

God Leads His Children

"For as many as are led by the Spirit of God, they are the sons of God" (Rom. 8:14).

"The LORD is my shepherd . . . he leadeth me beside the still waters . . . he leadeth me in the paths of righteousness for his name's sake" (Psa. 23:1-3).

Often it is difficult to make decisions, and it is not always easy to know the will of God. In such times it is well to remember that God leads His children. We just need to be patient and wait upon the Lord.

There are some things to remember about how God leads, or doesn't lead. The Spirit of God never leads us to do anything contrary to the Word of God, and He never leads us to do anything that is wrong. God leads us in paths of righteousness for His name's sake. God wants us to follow paths that will honor Him. Doing so will bring peace of mind and blessings from God.

May 15

We Have Today

"BOAST not thyself of to morrow; for thou knowest not what a day may bring forth" (Prov. 27:1).

Yesterday is gone, and tomorrow has not arrived. So we only have today. For many tomorrow will never come. This is a warning to the unsaved. The Bible tells us that today is the day of salvation. Tomorrow may be too late to be saved. We should do what we can to win the lost today.

Our text is also a warning to the children of God. Tomorrow it may be too late to say kind words to a loved one. Tomorrow it may be too late to make amends to an injured friend. Tomorrow it may be too late to confess a wrong and ask forgiveness.

This is a day that God has given us. How we spend it is largely up to us. We can spend the day in self-gratification, or we can spend it in the service of God and our fellowman.

We are on a journey from time to eternity, and today is only a tiny step toward that destination. We should use the day to the glory of God. We should take time to pray and worship God and to thank Him for all our blessings. We can endeavor to be a blessing to others. We can even perform long-neglected task.

May 16
The Blessed Life

"BLESSED is the man that walketh not in the counsel of the ungodly, nor standeth in the way of sinners, nor sitteth in the seat of the scornful. But his delight is in the law of the LORD; and in his law doth he meditate day and night. And he shall be like a tree planted by the rivers of water, that bringeth forth his fruit in his season; his leaf also shall not wither; and whatsoever he doeth shall prosper" (Psa. 1:1-3).

The Psalmist makes it clear that there are things

we should not do if we want to enjoy the blessings of God. Following the advice of the wrong role models is one of them. Being a bad testimony to the lost is another. Joining the company of scornful people is yet another. His warning should make us walk carefully before our God.

Further, the Psalmist tells us that delighting in the Word of God and meditating upon it will bring the blessing of God upon our lives. God will make us like a tree with leaves that never wither and fruit that never fails. Prospering in all that we do is another of God's blessings. It is our privilege to meditate upon God's Word and to walk in His ways. When we do we can claim the Lord's blessings.

May 17
Another Blessed Day

"This is the day which the LORD hath made; we will rejoice and be glad in it" (Psa. 118:24).

What a blessing it is to have another day to live! Yet, wonderful as it is to have this day, we can spoil it by having a bad attitude. Or we can enjoy it and help others enjoy it by having a good attitude. We can go through the day grumbling and complaining, or we can go through the day with gladness and rejoicing. The choice is ours.

Each day we have decisions to make and tasks to perform. We can make the decisions and perform the tasks joyfully, or we can we can go through the day grumbling and complaining. If we do that we will be miserable, and we will make others miserable. It is important that we let the Lord guide us in making our decisions. It is also important that we perform our tasks cheerfully.

In spite of the pressures of a busy life, we should take time to pray, and we should make this day and every future day a day of praise and rejoicing.

May 18
Dealing with Our Sins

"If we confess our sins, he is faithful and just to forgive us our sins, and to cleanse us from all unrighteousness" (1 John 1:9).

There are times when we say things or do things that we know are not right. When that happens we are not to become discouraged or to feel that we cannot live a Christian life. Instead, we are to ask for God's forgiveness. He has promised to forgive us and cleanse us from all unrighteousness.

Asking God to forgive us is our part. God's part is to forgive us. We are told that He is faithful. That means He is dependable. We are also told that He is just. Jesus has paid for our sins, and a just God will not require that we pay for them a second time. When we confess, God will forgive all our sins. We should make it a daily practice to confess our sins, even those that we do not realize that we have committed. That way there will be nothing between us and our God, and we can live victoriously.

May 19
Continual Cleansing

"But if we walk in the light, as he is in the light, we have fellowship one with another, and the blood of Jesus Christ his Son cleanseth us from all sin" (I John 1:7).

When we walk in the light of God's Word, we have fellowship with Him and with other Christians.

When we do not walk in the light, our fellowship is broken. So it is important that we walk in the light every day.

When we walk in the light, we have the promise of continual cleansing. Years ago the black gospel singer, Amanda Smith, told of something that happened before she became widely used in the Lord's work. One day when she was washing clothes in water from a spring branch that ran behind her house, she saw her little boy playing with a small, dirty rock. She took the rock from him and threw it in the branch. The next day she saw that the current of the branch had washed the dirty rock and made it clean. She said, "We can keep our lives in the currents of God's love, and we will always be washed clean."

May 20

It Pays to Serve Jesus

"For bodily exercise profiteth little: but godliness is profitable unto all things, having promise of the life that now is, and of that which is to come" (I Tim. 4:8).

The chorus of an old song begins, "It pays to serve Jesus, it pays every day." The Apostle Paul tells us that godly living is far more profitable than bodily exercise. It does pay to exercise, but godly living is of far greater value.

When we live right, we have the promise of God's blessings in the present life. For starters, we have the indwelling presence of the Holy Spirit. He is our comforter, guide, teacher, and prayer helper. We have the love of God in our hearts, and we have the promise that God will never leave us or forsake us.

Further, we have the promise of that which is to come. That includes the return of Christ, a reunion with loved ones who have gone on before, a home in the land of many mansions, and rewards for faithful service. We have reason to be glad and rejoice in the service of the Lord.

May 21
Worry Does Not Pay

"And Jesus answered and said unto her, Martha, Martha, thou art careful and troubled about many things: But one thing is needful . . ." (Luke 10:41, 42).

"But I would have you without carefulness [worry] *. . ."* (1 Cor. 7:32).

On one occasion when Jesus was visiting in the home of Martha, Mary, and Lazarus, Mary sat at His feet while Martha was busy preparing dinner. The Bible says that Martha *"was cumbered about much serving."* Finally she asked Jesus to tell Mary to help her. Instead, Jesus issued a mild rebuke. Mary sitting at His feet was far more important than the many small things than Martha was worrying about as she prepared their dinner.

There are many reasons why we should not worry. Worry and faith cannot coexist. Worry does not solve problems. Most of the things we worry about never happen. Worry destroys health and shortens life. Worry can age us prematurely. Worry makes us hard to live with. When we pray most of our worries go away,

May 22
Making Good Use of Our Time

"Redeeming the time, because the days are evil" (Eph. 5:16).

Paul uses the phrase, *"Redeeming the time,"* again in Colossians 4:5. *"Redeeming the time,"* means that we are to make the best use of our time.

Years ago I heard the outstanding Kentucky evangelist, Mordecai Ham, speak on this phrase. He said that in the center column of his Bible the phrase was translated, *"buying up opportunities."* The phrase is rendered the same way in the Amplified New Testament.

A. B. Simpson, in his book, *Days of Heaven On Earth,* points out that the two Greek words, *ion* and *kairon* literally mean, the opportunity.

Each day God gives us 24 hours to live. Most of us spend about a third of that time entertaining ourselves and sleeping. That leaves us 16 hours. We can easily spend 6 hours dressing, eating, and socializing. That leaves us with only 10 hours. Traveling to and from work and time spent on the job can easily take the remaining 10 hours. That leaves us no time to worship God or to be a blessing to others. Truly we must make the best use of all the time we have. *"Redeeming the time"* means that we should use our time carefully and wisely.

May 23

God Is With Us

"When thou passest through the waters, I will be with thee . . . " (Isa. 43:2).

God does not promise that we will never have trouble, but He does promise to be with us in trouble. The waters may roar, but they need not drown out the still small voice of our Lord. We have only to listen to hear His voice of comfort.

When we call upon God in times of trouble, He

answers, and in times of sorrow He is near. God comforts us in sorrow, gives strength in weakness, and guides us when our way is dark. When we are lonely it is well to remember that we are not alone, for He has promised never to leave us.

Worry Not

Worry not about tomorrow,
　　Nor fear the storm that may not come.
God is near in time of sorrow
　　Rest on Him till the race is run.

Troubled days are far outnumbered;
　　Brighter days slip quickly past.
But we need not be encumbered,
　　We will reach our home at last.

　　　　　　　　　　　—Louis Arnold

May 24
Walking in the Lord

"As ye have therefore received Christ Jesus the Lord, so walk ye in him" (Col. 2:6).

Unsaved people walk in the way of world. Only those who have received Jesus as Saviour can walk in Him. We are not simply to sit by the Lord or stand by the Lord, we are to walk in Him. As born again children of God, His Spirit dwells in us and enables us to walk in Him. *"For in him we live, and move, and have our being . . . For we are also his offspring"* (Acts 17:28).

Jesus was about His Father's business when He was only twelve. He asked His parents, *". . . wist ye not that I must be about my Father's business?"* (Luke 2:49). Just so, we should be about our Father's business.

We should never stop in our walk with the Lord.

It is too difficult to start again if we stop. Besides, if we stop we may block the paths of others.

We walked life's path alone before we knew the Lord. Now that we know Him, we should delight to walk with Him.

The Walk of Faith
I walked life's path alone,
   A way I had not gone before.
There were trials to me unknown,
   And pitfalls by the score.
Then I trusted in the Lord,
   And He said, "Come walk with me.
I'll guide you by my Word.
   Past dangers you do not see."

—Louis Arnold

May 25

God's Perfect Will

". . . be ye transformed by the renewing of your mind, that ye may prove what is that good, and acceptable, and perfect, will of God" (Rom. 12:2).

God has more than one will. First, God has a decreed will. Some things were decreed from eternity. These things will come to pass exactly as God has predetermined. For example, Jesus was born at the time and in the place God had predetermined.

Second, God has a directive will. He wants His children to walk in His directive will, but He will allow them to walk in the way of their own choosing. That is God's permissive will. When God's children walk in His permissive will they miss His greatest blessings, and they may incur His displeasure.

God directed Jonah to go to Nineveh, but He allowed him to get on a boat and start to Tarshish. Jonah got his way temporarily, but he paid for not doing what God directed him to do.

Further, God has a perfect will for each of His children. Our text speaks of the good, acceptable, and perfect will of God.

Our heavenly Father wants us to live in His perfect will. Walking in His will, we will do things that please Him, and we will be a blessing to others. In His perfect will we can enjoy the richest of His blessing and have our greatest success in life.

May 26

God's Loving Concern

"COMFORT ye, comfort ye my people, saith your God" (Isa. 40:1).

In D. L. Moody's early ministry he was pastor of a great church in Chicago. One day on church visitation, he found cause for distress in every home he visited. That made him realize that the world is full of trouble. That is true because sin is in the world. It was true in Isaiah's day when God gave him the message of comfort found in our text, and it is true today.

God wants us to know His comfort, and He wants us to comfort others. After we have gone through deep waters and have been comforted by God, we can empathize with those who are in trouble, and we can comfort them.

As a small boy, when I hurt myself, I would run to my mother, and she would take me in her arms and hold me until I forgot my pain. When I was older, I thought I was too big to run to my mother for comfort, so I suffered alone.

Grown-up people need to run to the Lord when they hurt. There they will find comfort, and they will learn how to comfort others who are in trouble or sorrow.

May 27

The Rock of Deliverance

". . . neither is there any rock like our God" (1 Sam. 2:2).

Years ago a lady told how her little son and another small boy got trapped in the woods by a forest fire. She stood weeping with some neighbors at the edge of the burning forest, waiting for the fire to burn itself out. She expected that they would only find the charred remains of the little boys when the ground cooled enough for them to search for them. But to her great joy the boys were found alive and safe.

"Weren't you frightened when you saw the woods on fire?" she asked her son as she clasped him in her arms.

"No, Mama, I wasn't afraid," he replied. "We got on top of old Chimney Rock. We knew the fire couldn't reach us there." God is our rock of safety.

In one of my meetings, an elderly preacher related the following story: A lady in West Virginia was fishing in Gauley River. She waded out in the river and climbed on top of a large rock to fish. A hard rain had fallen up the river, and the water where she was fishing started rising. Before she realized what was happening, she was trapped on the rock.

No one found her, and she had to spend the night on the rock with raging waves swirling around her. Only after the river ran down was she able to get off the rock and wade back to the riverbank. In relating the story she said: "I shook with fear all night, but the rock did not shake at all."

The Rock That Is Higher Than I

O sometimes the shadows are deep,
  And rough seems the path to the goal,
And sorrows, sometimes how they sweep
  Like tempests down over the soul!
O sometimes how long seems the day,
  And sometimes how weary my feet;
But toiling in life's dusty way,
  The Rock's blessed shadow, how sweet!
O near to the Rock let me keep,
  If blessings or sorrows prevail,
Or climbing the mountain way steep,
  Or walking the shadowy vale.

——E. Johnson

May 28

Being an Example

"For I know him, that he will command his children and his household after him, and they shall keep the way of the LORD . . ." (Gen. 18:19).

God knew Abraham and trusted him to train his children and his household in the way of the Lord. It is not enough that we live for God, we are responsible for the rearing of our children. We should set an example for them. We should lead them to trust Jesus as their Saviour at an early age, and we should teach them to serve Him.

Children should not be left to make up their own minds about serving the Lord. The devil will not let them make up their own minds. He will do everything possible to cause them to choose a life of sin.

Training our children to serve the Lord includes starting early, setting a godly example, praying for them faithfully, giving them godly counsel, and keeping them in church where they will hear the Gospel.

May 29
Making a Difference

"And of some have compassion, making a difference" (Jude 22).

We live in a troubled world. Many people are hurting, and many are unsaved. We are not placed in the world just to take care of ourselves and to entertain ourselves. We are here to make a difference in the lives of others. When we leave this world, it should be a better place because we lived to make a difference.

In the Gospels we often read that Jesus was moved with compassion, or we find Him saying, *"I have compassion on the multitude."* That simply means that Jesus cared.

All people do not have compassion. There are those who care only for themselves and live only for themselves. The people who care for others are the ones who make a difference.

If we are going to make a difference in this world, we must care for others, and we must give of our time, our money, our love, and our talents.

After a man who had lived a self-centered life had died, someone asked, "How much did he leave?" Someone who knew him replied, "He left it all." How much better it will be when we leave this world if it can be truly said, "They left a lifetime of blessings."

May 30
Secure in God's Love

"Who shall separate us from the love of Christ? shall tribulation, or distress, or persecution, or famine, or nakedness, or peril, or sword? Nay, in all these

things we are more than conquerors through him that loved us" (Rom. 8:35, 37).

Paul had experienced more than his share of trouble. He had been imprisoned, beaten, stoned, and shipwrecked. From his trials he had learned that nothing can separate us from the love of Christ.

Things go wrong with all of us at times, but we will never have as many troubles as Paul had. Even if we did, they would not separate us from the love of Christ.

God loves us as much when we are down as He does when we are on top of the world. God loved Elijah as much when he was under the juniper tree, discouraged and wanting to die, as He did when he was on Mt. Carmel praying fire out of Heaven. We are secure in God's love.

May 31
Jesus Cares

"And there arose a great storm of wind, and the waves beat into the ship, so that it was now full" (Mark 4:37).

Conditions could not have been worse for the disciples. They were in a small boat; it was night; it was storming; the boat was about to sink; and Jesus was asleep.

They may have questioned why they were in trouble. It was not because they were out of the Lord's will. They were doing exactly what the Lord had told them to do. He had said, *". . . Let us pass over unto the other side"* (Mark 4:35). That meant that they were to cross the Sea of Galilee in a small boat, and that was what they were doing. Jesus was in the ship with them, but that did not keep them from running into the storm.

The disciples were frightened, but Jesus did not appear to be concerned. He was sleeping through the storm. It is little wonder that they awoke Him and demanded, *". . . Master, carest thou not that we perish?"* (Mark 4:38).

They did not understand that Jesus had led them into the storm because He did care. He wanted to teach them to trust Him even when conditions appeared to be beyond control. He wanted them to know that He was master of the wind and the waves, and He wanted to show them that He could take care of them in times of trouble.

People in all ages can learn this lesson. When the storms of life are beyond our control, we can call upon the One who is the master of the storms.

Devotions for June

June 1
God Is Near

"GOD is our refuge and strength, a very present help in trouble" (Psa. 46:1).

A refuge is a place of shelter and protection, but it is of no value when trouble comes if it is not nearby. It is comforting to know that God is a present help in trouble. That means that He is always near and that He will hear and answer our prayers.

In Jeremiah 33:3 we read, *"Call unto me, and I will answer thee, and shew thee great and mighty things, which thou knowest not."*

In our text for today we are told that God is our refuge. That means that He is our shelter when storms come. There are times when a shelter is a necessity, but it is only useful when we take advantage of it.

When I was a small boy I went camping with my parents at our favorite place on Dix River, a few miles from Lancaster, Kentucky. When bedtime came we bedded down on a large flat rock near the river. Almost at once we heard thunder and saw zigzag lightning dancing across the sky. A brisk wind started fanning the leaves on the tree above us, and large raindrops started splattering on the rocks. I was frightened, for I thought there was no way for us to escape the storm.

"There's a cave a short distance from here where we can shelter," my father said as he bounded out of bed.

I jumped out of bed, and my mother also got up. We gathered up our bedclothes, and my father led the way up the riverbank to the cave. We all ran inside just as the rain started pouring. The storm lasted all night, but we were safe and dry. We had found a shelter in a time of storm.

We have no promise that we can avoid the storms of life, but we do have the promise that God will be our shelter when the storms of trouble and sorrow come our way.

June 2

The Valley of Blessings

"Who passing through the valley of Baca make it a well; the rain also filleth the pools" (Psa. 84:6).

The Valley of Baca stretches between the ruins of the ancient city of Beirut, Lebanon and the mountains. On one of my visits to the Holy Land our guide showed us this valley and told us that it was one of the most fertile and productive valleys in the region. He went on to say that an underground river flowed beneath the valley.

"Dig down two feet anywhere in this valley and you will find water, but there is no water to be found in the mountains that border the valley," he told us.

The picture is clear. Our text tells us that we must pass through the valley to find the well and the overflowing pools. So it is in our walk with the Lord. In the center of His will we enjoy His blessings. Out of His will we miss His blessings. The blessings of the Lord are like a river that never runs dry. When we stay in His will, we get the blessings. If we get out of His will, we miss His blessings. Though Baca is a valley, we should not go around it. We should pass through it, for that is where God's blessings flow.

June 3

Cause to Rejoice

"He turned the sea into dry land: they went through the flood on foot: there did we rejoice in him" (Psa. 66:6).

The writers of the Bible often recalled great things God had done in the past. The Holy Spirit must have inspired these writers to recall these events to encourage God's people in times of discouragement.

In our text for today we are told that God turned the sea into dry land. That was a miracle. The people went through the flood on foot. That was another miracle. The people could have been weary and discouraged, but they passed safely through the sea.

The great things God did in the past were evidences that He lives, and that He is a God of power. His miracles gave the people cause to rejoice. Even to this day, when we read these accounts in the Bible, our faith is renewed, and we have cause to rejoice.

Recognizing that God lives, that He is almighty, and that He cares for His own gives us cause to worship. A good portion of our prayer time should be spent in worshiping and praising the Lord.

June 4

Overcoming Depression

"Why art thou cast down, O my soul? and why art thou disquieted within me? hope in God . . ." (Psa. 43:5).

The writer of this Psalm was dismayed that his soul, the very seat of his emotions, was downcast. Further, he was troubled that he was disquieted. To be disquieted is to have an absence of peace or rest.

As obedient Christians we should not be depressed, but sometimes we are. Sometimes, like the Psalmist, we question why we are depressed. When we know we have done nothing to cause distress of mind, depression can be really troubling.

The writer of this Psalm, as far as we know, did not learn why he was depressed, but he did find a solution. It was, *"Hope in God,"* he exulted. Just so, when we are troubled, we can look to God in faith.

Being downcast may come from a variety of causes. Depression can be caused by Satan; it may have a physical origin; it may be caused by doubt; it may be because of circumstances over which we have no control; it may be caused by the presence of a depressing individual; or it may be caused by any number of other things. But, no matter what the cause, we can hope in God. Make God your hope, and have a good day in spite of whatever is troubling you.

June 5

Giving Our Best Each Day

"I must work the works of him that sent me, while it is day: the night cometh, when no man can work" (John 9:4).

Every day opportunities pass our way. That was true in Jesus' day, and it is true in our day. Some opportunities will not return. If we are to take advantage of them, we must do so today.

Each sunrise brings the promise of a new day with potential blessings, opportunities, and challenges. It is well to start the day wondering what blessing the Lord will bring our way and what opportunities we will have to be a blessing to others.

Each day offers opportunities to serve the Lord. We can serve Him by letting our light shine. We can serve Him by witnessing to the lost. We can serve Him by refusing to be led into sin, and we can serve Him by encouraging others to make the right choices. When we follow the path of God's leading we will be an example to others.

June 6

Perfect Peace

"Thou wilt keep him in perfect peace, whose mind is stayed on thee: because he trusteth in thee. Trust ye in the LORD for ever . . ." (Isa. 26:3, 4).

Years ago I visited in the home of a church family in a community where I was holding a meeting. While the wife was cooking dinner the husband and I sat in the living room talking. After a while he pointed to the picture on the wall of a handsome young man in uniform.

"That was our only son, and he died in combat while serving in the army overseas," he said.

"That was a terrible loss," I sympathized. "How did you and your wife ever adjust to it?"

"We just stayed on the Lord," he replied.

That was a unique way to put it, but I understood what he meant. Perhaps he had our text from Isaiah in mind.

In this world few things are permanent enough for us to depend upon, and nothing in the world is able to keep us in perfect peace. Only God can do that. Whatever our problems are today, we can still trust the Lord to keep us in perfect peace.

June 7

The Humble Walk

". . . and what doth the LORD require of thee, but to do justly, and to love mercy, and to walk humbly with thy God?" (Mic. 6:8).

There are three things in this text that God requires of His children. He requires that we do justly, that we love mercy, and that we walk humbly with Him. To do justly is to be honest and fair in our dealings. That includes paying our debts when they come due. When it is not possible to pay on time, the creditor should be contacted, given an explanation, and told when we expect to be able to pay.

To love mercy means that we are to have a forgiving spirit. It also means that we are to be sympathetic with others when they are in trouble and do kindness to them when possible.

Finally, we are to walk humbly with our God. That means we are not to have a haughty spirit. We need to realize that all we have and all that we are we owe to Him.

A careful reading of this verse shows that we are greatly blessed. We are not just to walk before our God, we are privileged to walk with Him. In this exalted position we should walk humbly.

June 8

Walking by Faith

"And it shall come to pass, as soon as the soles of the feet of the priests . . . shall rest in the waters of Jordan . . . the waters of Jordan shall be cut off . . . and they shall stand upon an heap" (Josh. 3:13).

The people of Israel had spent forty years wandering in the wilderness. At last they were encamped near the Jordan River, ready to cross into the Promised Land. The river was overflowing its banks, but, instead of waiting for the water to run down, they broke camp and made ready to cross.

The priests led the way, carrying the ark of the covenant, and the people followed. The rushing water did not slow as the people walked toward the river, so it took faith to continue to walk toward it. The river did not stop until the feet of the priest touched the water.

There is a lesson here. We often expect results before we put our faith to work. Instead of complaining when the water did not slow down, the people marched on. God usually leads us one step at a time. Even when we cannot see where our pathway is leading, we should continue to walk by faith.

June 9

Looking to the Hills

"I WILL lift up mine eyes unto the hills, from whence cometh my help" (Psa. 121:1).

Animals were created with eyes that look outward and downward. Man was created with eyes that look outward and upward. When we pray or worship, we often lift our eyes toward the heavens.

Our heavenly Father is the God of the hills and of the valleys, but we lift our eyes to the hills when we need His help. No animal ever prays for its baby or for itself. Only man was created with a longing for God in his heart, and only man looks upward to God for help. Even unsaved people pray. Heathen people who have never heard the Gospel pray, though they know not to whom they are praying. The need to pray is a built in longing for help from a higher power.

It is wonderful that we can pray in the name of

Jesus, knowing that He hears and answers prayer.

June 10

The Trees Shall Clap Their Hands

". . . the mountains and the hills shall break forth before you into singing, and all the trees of the field shall clap their hands" (Isa. 55:12).

In the context of this verse God speaks of the rain and the snow that comes upon the earth and makes it productive. Then He tells us that His Word will bring forth a harvest of joy and a time of peace. So great will be the blessing that mountains and hills will break forth with singing and the trees shall clap their hands.

This is a prophecy of the glorious millennial age, but it can have a present application. When unsaved people receive Jesus as their Saviour, that is cause for joy. Figuratively speaking, the heart of a new-born person can clap its hands for joy. Unsaved people know no such joy. They can do no better than speak of having fun or getting a thrill. Christians can have joy unspeakable and full of glory.

June 11

The High Places

"And I will make all my mountains a way, and my highways shall be exalted" (Isa. 49:11).

We speak of being on the mountaintop when all is going well or down in the valley when things go wrong. We would like to be on the mountaintop all the time, but we all have to go through our valleys. Valleys are times of testing. In the valley we have to walk by faith. Someone has said, "When the outlook is not good, try the up-look.

Faith, meditation, and prayer will help us get out of our valleys and start toward the mountaintop. Being active in the Lord's work will help even more. We often speak of climbing the ladder of success. Dr. B. R. Lakin used to say, "Be nice to those you pass on the way up. You may meet them on your way back down."

Our text speaks of the exalted highway. The Bible also speaks of the King's highway, and it speaks of the wrong highway. *"There is a way that seemeth right unto a man, but the end thereof are the ways of death"* (Prov. 16:25). The King's highway begins at the cross and ends in the glory world. Only after we are on that highway can we travel the exalted highway.

June 12
Keeping in Touch

"Pray without ceasing" (I Thess. 5:17).

The prophet, Daniel, prayed morning, noon, and night with his window open toward Jerusalem. Jesus prayed often. Sometimes He prayed all night. He prayed before every important event in His life. He even prayed when He was dying on the cross.

Many Christians pray at night. Some pray morning and night. Others pray as they go about their daily tasks or when they are alone in their cars. That is approaching the idea of praying without ceasing.

Praying without ceasing does not mean that we are to be constantly praying aloud. Prayers can be whispered or even expressed in the mind. Praying without ceasing means that we are constantly in touch with God.

People can spend pleasant hours together without being in constant conversation. Yet, when asked what they have been doing, they say, "We have been talking." They were in communion even during the periods of silence. In like manner we can be in constant communion with God.

June 13
God's Protection

". . . greater is he that is in you, than he that is in the world" (1 John 4:4).

Some people have a Satan complex. They blame their slightest problem on Satan. Instead of trusting in the Lord, they are constantly watching to see what Satan will do next.

Satan is in the world, and he is our enemy. Paul wrote about Satan hindering him and his helpers, and Peter wrote about Satan walking about as a roaring lion. That is enough to frighten any Christian, but we must remember that the Holy Spirit is in our hearts, and that He who is in us is greater than Satan.

Satan wanted to sift Peter as wheat is sifted, and Jesus prayed that his faith would not fail. When Satan tempted Jesus, He commanded him to go away, and Satan had to obey.

What are we to do when Satan tries to defeat us? We are not to fear him. Instead, we are to look to Jesus and let Him handle Satan. Jesus can give us victory over Satan. That means that we do not have to live in fear of what Satan will do.

June 14
God Directed Footsteps

"Trust in the LORD with all thine heart; and lean not unto thine own understanding. In all thy ways acknowledge him, and he shall direct thy paths" (Prov. 3:5, 6).

There is nothing simple about our lives. We have many interests, many responsibilities, and many choices to make. It is easy, even natural, to lean to our own understanding when making our choices. When we do, we depend on our own wisdom (or lack of wisdom) to direct our paths. That is why we so often make mistakes that get us in trouble. The solution is to trust in God and seek His direction in all our decisions. When God's direction is not immediately clear, we need to be patient and wait until the way is made clear. Sometimes God leads by an impression upon the heart that grows stronger with the passing of time. Other times God leads by opened and closed doors. Sometimes He leads by unexpected and unusual coincidences. The secret of finding His leadership is to trust in Him, to acknowledge Him, and to wait upon Him.

June 15

God Feeds the Sparrows

"Behold the fowls of the air . . . your heavenly Father feedeth them . . ." (Matt. 6:26).

In the sermon on the mount, Jesus told His hearers not to worry about physical needs such as food and clothing. He told them that the lilies were more beautifully arrayed than King Solomon in all his glory, and He reminded them that God feeds the birds. That means that we are to trust in God and not worry.

Years ago, on the way to my office at the church I was pastoring, I stopped at the post office for my mail. While I was there, I heard two businessmen talking about hard times. They were convinced that we were headed into the greatest depression of all time. According to them, hard times were just around the corner.

I was greatly depressed when I left the post office and started driving toward the church. When I turned into the driveway that led to the parking lot of the church, I saw some sparrows chirping in a thicket. My first thought was, *Those stupid birds do not know a great depression is coming.* Then I realized how stupid my thought was. God would continue to feed the sparrow just as He always had. The economy of our country had nothing to do with God's supply. I then realized that God would take care of me just as He was taking care of the sparrows. My spirits lifted, and I went to my office on shouting ground.

June 16

God Will Supply

"I have been young, and now am old; yet have I not seen the righteous forsaken, nor his seed begging bread" (Psa. 37:25).

On my second series of meetings in the Bahamas, an old man called me over to where he was sitting and gave the following testimony.

"I am old and have no way to make a living, but since I got saved in your meeting last year, God has been taking care of me. I have a couple of old hens, and they keep me in eggs. Some days neighbors bring me fish they have caught from the sea or some fruit and vegetables they have gathered. Other days some tourists buy seashells that have been given to me, and I am able to buy food. One way or another, God is taking care of me." I was so impressed by his testimony that I wrote the following poem about him.

God Will Supply

A gray old man lived all alone
With not a thing to call his own.
When someone asked how he got by,
"I trust in God," was his reply.

"I once was young, I now am old.
God will supply I've oft' been told.
God will supply; He feeds the birds.
I've read it in His holy Word."

"But aren't you lonely?" someone asked.
"And don't you tire from all your tasks?"
"My God is near," was his reply.
"He meets all needs, so I'll get by."

"But what when summer's flowers fade,
And no one comes to give you aid?"
"God cares for me," was his reply.
"His Word can't fail, so I'll get by.

—Louis Arnold

June 17

Turning Trials into Blessings

"Knowing this, that the trying of your faith worketh patience" (James 1:3).

In the early part of the last century, the great black preacher and songwriter, C. A. Tindley, wrote a wonderful song because of a trial he experienced.

He traveled many miles with his wife to hold a revival in a church. When the meeting closed the love offering was only enough to pay his wife's fare home on the train.

After he had seen her off on the train with their meager baggage, he started walking the railroad tracks toward home. He was tired and discouraged, but as he walked, he started making up the words and melody of a song. When he had finished the first verse, he sang:

"If the world from you withholds of its silver and its gold,
And you have to get along with meager fare,
Just remember, in His word, how He feeds the little bird;
Take your burden to the Lord and leave it there."

As the old preacher continued walking the tracks he made up the second and third verses and sang.

"If your body suffers pain and your health you can't regain,
And your soul is almost sinking in despair,
Jesus knows the pain you feel. He can save and He can heal;
Take your burden to the Lord and leave it there.
"When your enemies assail, and your heart begins to fail,
Don't forget that God in Heaven answers prayer;
He will make a way for you, and will lead you safely thro'.
Take your burden to the Lord and leave it there."

As the old preacher continued walking the railroad ties, thoughts of better days filled his mind. He was tired and weary, but soon he was singing:

"When your youthful days are gone and old age is stealing on,
And your body bends beneath the weight of care;
He will never leave you then, He'll go with you to the end.
Take your burden to the Lord and leave it there."

Chorus:

"Leave it there, leave it there,
Take your burden to the Lord and leave it there;
If you trust and never doubt,
He will surely bring you out;
Take your burden to the Lord and leave it there."

By the time the old preacher reached home, he had turned his trial into blessings, and the song he wrote has been a blessing to multitudes of tired, weary, discouraged people through the years.

June 18
Faith to Live By

". . . The just shall live by faith" (Rom. 1:17).

Faith is positive. Doubt is negative. We are not supposed to live by doubt. We are supposed to live by faith. Yet many good Christians live on the negative side. They are always down in the dumps, always worrying about something, and always complaining.

Just as light drives away darkness, faith drives away fear and worry, but we may still have a problem. Doubt can creep back into the heart and struggle with faith. All too often doubt makes us become negative again. When that happens we need to strengthen our faith. Reading the Word of God is the way to do that. *"So then faith cometh by hearing, and hearing by the word of God"* (Rom. 10:17).

Following is a list of things that will help us stay on the positive side:

1. Remember that God lives.
2. Remember that God is all powerful.
3. Remember that God is our Father.
4. Remember that God loves us.

5. Remember that God wants the best for us.
6. Remember that God answers prayer.

June 19

What to Do with Burdens

"Cast thy burden upon the LORD, and he shall sustain thee: he shall never suffer the righteous to be moved" (Psa. 55:22).

We all have our burdens, and sometimes they seem more than we can bear. Often we struggle beneath their weight, forgetting that we are told to cast them upon the Lord.

There is the story of a man who was carrying a heavy sack on his shoulders. A neighbor stopped his wagon and invited him to ride. The man climbed aboard, but he did not set down his heavy load.

"Why don't you put down your sack?" the neighbor asked.

"It is so good of you to let me ride, I can't think of asking you to carry my sack also," the man replied.

It is well to remember that the Lord wants to carry our burdens. The burdens that seem so heavy to us are as nothing to the Lord. The One who scooped out the ocean beds with His mighty hand, piled the mountain ranges toward the sky, spread out the fertile plains, and covered the deserts with sand is certainly able to bear our tiny burdens.

June 20

Keep on Praying

". . . . Ask, and it shall be given you; seek, and ye shall find; knock, and it shall be opened unto you" (Luke 11:9).

This text contains some directions and some promises. We are told to ask, to seek, and to knock.

We are promised that we will receive when we ask, find when we seek, and that closed doors will be opened when we knock.

Dr. John Rice, in his book on prayer, states that "Prayer is asking, and answered prayer is receiving." God is in the prayer answering business, but He does not always answer our prayers in the same way. Sometimes He answers while we are yet speaking. Other times we have to wait for the answer. Then there are times when God sees fit to deny our prayer and give us something better. For example, Paul prayed three times for the thorn in his flesh to be removed, but his request was denied. Instead, God gave him added grace.

Sometimes we only have to ask, and the prayer is answered. Other times we have to seek. That may include searching our own hearts to see if we are hindering the answer to our prayers. Other times we may have to climb a ladder of travail to the very gate of Heaven and knock on the gate. In other words, we must have a burning desire and make a passionate appeal before our prayer is answered. The message of our text is that we are to keep on praying until the answer comes.

June 21

Rest Without Worry

"I will both lay me down in peace, and sleep: for thou, LORD, only makest me dwell in safety" (Psa. 4:8).

Many have the habit of taking their troubles to bed with them. Instead of sleeping they roll and toss and worry through the night. The night of worry does not drive their troubles away, and the next day will not be a good one.

Years ago I was facing some church problems that were almost driving me out of my mind, and I was taking the problems to bed with me. One night as I knelt by my bed with my Bible before me, the Bible fell open to the fourth Psalm, and my eyes fell upon the eighth verse, (our text for today). The verse spoke to my heart, and I turned my problem over to the Lord. I got into bed and slept through the night without a care. God soon solved my problem without my help, and I realized that all my worry had been in vain.

Through the years when facing problems I have turned to this text again and again. Always the text has given me faith to leave the solution of the problem in God's hands, and that has enabled me to say, *"I will both lay me down in peace, and sleep: for thou, LORD, only makest me dwell in safety."*

June 22

There Is a Price to Pay

". . . neither will I offer burnt-offerings unto the LORD my God of that which doth cost me nothing . . . " (2 Sam. 24:24).

In this day of gadgets and switches we do things the easy way. This has become a way of life, so it is not strange that we want to serve the Lord with little effort as possible.

In a time of crisis the prophet, Gad, told King David to offer burnt offerings on a threshing floor that belonged to Araunah. Araunah offered to give the threshing floor to the King without costs and to donate oxen and wood for the burnt offering. But David refused the offer, saying that he would not worship God with that which had cost him nothing.

Salvation is a gift of God. It cost us nothing to be saved, but it does cost us to serve God. There are costs that we all should pay. Among these are the following:

1. We should pay the price of separation. After we receive Jesus as our Saviour we should separate ourselves from the sinful practices of the world.

2. We should pay the price of dedication. We should serve the Lord with all that we have and all that we are. Jesus' hands and feet were nailed to the cross. That means that He bought our hands and our feet. So we should walk with Him and work for Him. His brow was crowned with thorns, and His heart was broken. He bought our heads and our hearts. So we should love Him and be thankful to Him.

3. We should pay the price of supplication. That means praying for others. Job was not delivered from his troubles when he prayed only for himself. The Lord delivered him when he prayed for his friends (Job 42:10).

4. We should pay the price of application. That means using time, talents, energy, and possessions to the glory of God. Let us say with King David, *"Neither will I offer burnt-offerings unto the LORD my God of that which cost me nothing."*

June 23

When Your Load Is Heavy

". . . as thy days, so shall thy strength be" (Deut. 33:25).

What a marvelous promise. The children of Israel were in a wilderness where they were destined to wander for forty years. God was feeding them with manna from Heaven. He caused their garments not to wear out, and He promised to give them strength for every day of their journey.

God does not lead us for a lifetime in advance, or even for a year. He leads us one day at a time.

When I was a boy, growing up on the farm, I often went hunting with my dogs at night. I carried an oil lantern to light my way. On such a hunt, I often walked five or ten miles, but the lantern did not light the entire way at once.

When I left the house, the lantern only cast a circle of light a few steps in front of me, but when I started walking the circle of light moved with me, and the lantern lighted the entire distance of my hunt. Darkness was around me all the way, but I never walked in darkness.

Just so, the Lord lights our pathway one step at a time. Darkness may surround us, but we need not walk in darkness. The Lord has promised never to leave us. No matter how dark our way may be, He will be with us and give us strength for the journey.

June 24

There Is Comfort For You

"Blessed be God, even the Father of our Lord Jesus Christ, the Father of mercies, and the God of all comfort" (2 Cor. 1:3).

In times of sorrow, we need a comforter. Human comforters can help, but only God can heal a broken heart. Good memories help to comfort us, but they alone cannot heal our hurt. Someone has said, "Sorrow last only for a season, but memories last for a lifetime." Memories are great comforters, but God is a greater comforter.

Not long before Jesus was to be crucified, He told

His disciples that He was going away. Then He told them that He would not leave them without comfort but that He would send the Holy Spirit to be their comforter. *"And I will pray the Father, and he shall give you another Comforter, that he may abide with you for ever"* (John 14:16).

During my years as a pastor I often witnessed the comforting work of the Holy Spirit. When trying to comfort a grieving family members who had lost a loved one, I made it a practice to pray for the Holy Spirit to comfort them. Without fail, I always saw an immediate change in the person's demeanor and outlook.

Our God is the God of all comfort, and He will never fail us.

June 25

Worry Does Not Help

"Therefore I say unto you, Take no thought for your life, what ye shall eat, or what ye shall drink; nor yet for your body, what ye shall put on..." (Matt. 6:25).

Some people are born worriers. They worry about things that never happen. They worry when all is going well. They worry when they have everything they need. Then, when real trouble comes, they have not learned to cast their care upon the Lord.

While I was doing mission work in the Bahamas, a native told me a story that contains a powerful message. He said, "A man was worrying because he had nothing but one banana to eat. He feared that after it was gone he would starve. Finally he decided to climb far up in a coconut tree and eat his banana, then to jump out of the tree and kill himself.

"He climbed the tree, peeled the banana, and threw down the peeling. While he was eating the banana, another man came walking down the path, swinging his arms and singing. When he came to the banana peeling, he picked it up, brushed away the dirt, and ate it. Then he continued down the path swinging his arms and singing.

"The man in the tree realized that there were others worse off than he was, and he decided to climb back down the tree and go on with his life." Perhaps the singing man had caused him to remember that the God who feeds the sparrow would take care of him.

June 26

What to Do When Things Go Wrong

"We are troubled on every side, yet not distressed; we are perplexed, but not in despair" (2 Cor. 4:8).

The Apostle Paul and his co-workers faced every kind of trial imaginable. He wrote that they were troubled on every side, perplexed, persecuted, and cast down. Then he added, *"Yet not distressed."* That raises a question. How was it possible for him to be upbeat when everything that was happening was downbeat?

The meaning of the word distress is, "To cause strain, anxiety, or suffering." Paul and his co-workers were certainly experiencing all of that, but they were not distressed. The archaic meaning of distress is, "To constrain or to overcome by harassment." They were certainly constrained and harassed, but they were not distressed. They had victory. We too can have victory when things go wrong. Faith is our victory.

During the fourth century, Chrysostom was summoned before the Emperor Arcadius and threatened with banishment. He is reported to have replied: "Thou canst not banish me, for the world is my Father's house."

"Then I will slay thee," the emperor threatened.

"Nay, but thou canst not, for my life is hid with Christ in God."

"Your treasures will be confiscated," was the next threat.

"Sire, that cannot be. My treasures are in Heaven, as my heart is there."

"But I will drive thee from men, and thou shalt have no friends left."

"That you cannot do either, Sire. I have a friend in Heaven who has said, 'I will never leave thee nor forsake thee'."

Chrysostom had victory through faith. When Christ is real to us we can also have victory through faith no matter how great our trials.

June 27

The Blessing of Giving

"*. . . It is more blessed to give than to receive*" (Acts 20:35).

That which we receive, whether it be a gift or in payment for services rendered, can only bless us for a limited time. That which we give in the name of Christ will bless us for time and eternity. Giving brings satisfaction in this life and a reward in the life to come. Whether we give of our means or of ourselves, the principle is the same. "*. . . It is more blessed to give than to receive.*"

Giving is like sowing seed. We give the seed to

the ground, and the ground brings forth a harvest. The harvest is larger than the amount of seed we sow. When we give to others we enrich their lives, and they have the opportunity to pass on the blessing to others.

When we give for the Lord's work, the blessing may touch the lives of many we have never seen. We will never know how many lives our giving has blessed until we reach the glory world. Then we will truly understand that *". . . It is more blessed to give than it is to receive."*

June 28

Light in a Dark World

"Ye are the light of the world . . ." (Matt. 5:14). *". . . ye shine as lights in the world" (*Phil. 2:15)

This is a dark world. Jesus said, *". . . men loved darkness rather than light, because their deeds were evil"* (John 3:19).

When Jesus was born, midnight blossomed into the light of day. Light had come into the world. The day Jesus died on the cross, day darkened into midnight. Light had gone out of the world.

While Jesus was in the world, He was the Light of the world. When He left the world, He left His church to be the light of the world. Individual believers are to shine as lights.

In Genesis 1:16 we have the record an actual event, but the verse also contains a wonderful type. It tells us, *"And God made two great lights; the greater light to rule the day, and the lesser light to rule the night: he made the stars also."*

The greater light is the sun. It is a type of the Son

of God. The lesser light is the moon. It is a type of the church. As the moon shines by reflecting the light of the sun, the church shines by reflecting the light of the Son of God. The stars are a type of individual believers. That means that each one of us is to be a light in this dark world. What a challenge that is. The only light that many of the lost ever see is the light of Christ shining through us. We should let our light shine for the Lord every day.

June 29

God Knows Your Needs

". . . your heavenly Father knoweth that ye have need of all these things" (Matt. 6:32).

Why should we pray about our needs when God already knows what we need? We should pray because God wants us to have fellowship with Him. Further, we should pray so we will know the source of our supply.

We should not think of God as a kind of celestial coin machine. When we put a coin in a machine and get something in return, we could not care less about the machine. When we put in a prayer and get something in return, we should never think that God is not important. Prayer is not only asking, prayer is worship, praise and fellowship. Each time we pray should bring us closer to God.

God often supplies our needs before we ask. When that happens, we should offer a prayer of thanksgiving. Sometimes God doesn't supply our needs right away. When that happens, we should continue to pray—and to trust. *"And let us not be weary in well doing: for in due season we shall reap, if we faint not"* (Gal. 6:9).

June 30

First Things First

"But seek ye first the kingdom of God, and his righteousness; and all these things shall be added unto you" (Matt. 6:33).

It is well to ask ourselves, what is my first thought when I wake up in the morning? and what is my last thought before I fall asleep at night? If we would seek God and His kingdom first, we would not have to spend so much time thinking about things we need or want.

There are many things that can become first in our lives. Without realizing it, money, friends, popularity, entertainment, travel, hobbies, etc., can become first. None of these are wrong unless they become so important that we have no time for God.

That which is first in our lives can become an object of worship, and God tells us that we are to have no other gods before Him.

God knows that we have need of things, and He has promised to supply them. He just doesn't want us to put material things ahead of Him.

Devotions for July

July 1
The Ministry of Helps

"And God hath set some in the church ... helps ... " (1 Cor. 12:28).

The ministry of helps may be hardly noticed, but it is a ministry that is important to God. In a list of ministries given in our verse for today, the lowly ministry of helps is listed with teachers, miracles, healing, governments, and diversities of tongues.

Helps is not at the end of the list, neither is it the beginning. The ministry of helps does not put itself on parade or claimer for recognition. It does its important work quietly.

Helps can be assisting an overburdened leader. Helps can be assisting those who are ill or handicapped. Helps can share the burden of one who is overburdened with cares, and on and on. Helps looks for an opportunity to serve. Those who serve in the ministry of helps may, for all we know, have the richest rewards in Heaven.

July 2
Sons of God

"Beloved, now are we the sons of God ... " (1 John 3:2).

". . . that we might receive the adoption of sons" (Gal. 4:5).

Jesus is the only begotten Son of God, but God has many sons. Angels are created sons of God. Saved people are born-again sons and daughters of God. When we receive Jesus as our Saviour, we are born into the family of God. Jesus becomes our elder brother, and we become joint heirs with Him.

We are also the children of God by adoption. Our bodies have not been born again, but they will be adopted. Paul writes, *". . . we ourselves groan within ourselves, waiting for the adoption, to wit, the redemption of our body"* (Rom. 8:23).

There is no way the devil can contest the fact that we are the children of God. We are His children both by birth and by adoption. That is shouting ground. Jesus is our Saviour; God is our Father; saved people are our brothers and sisters; the church is our sphere of service, and Heaven is our home. Knowing all that should fill our hearts with joy.

July 3

Affliction Brings Reward

"For our light affliction, which is but for a moment, worketh for us a far more exceeding and eternal weight of glory" (2 Cor. 4:17).

Our affliction may sometimes seem heavy, but Paul calls them light afflictions. They are light because they only last for a moment when compared to eternity. They are light when compared to the sufferings of Jesus on the cross. They are light when compared to the sufferings of others.

Often our affliction may seem especially bad because we do not understand why we are suffering. The following poem, entitled, *The Weaving,* can be a source of comfort.

The Weaving

My life is but a weaving
Between my God and me.
I may but choose the colors;
He worketh steadily.

Full oft' He worketh sorrow,
And I in foolish pride
Forget He sees the upper
And I the under side.

The dark threads are as needful,
In the skillful weaver's hands
As the threads of gold and silver
In the pattern He has planned.

Not until the loom is silent,
And the shuttles cease to fly,
Will God unfold the canvas
And explain the reason why.

—Author Unknown

Paul tells us that our troubles will bring an eternal weight of glory. That is a reward we will not have to work for. Let us rejoice and be glad, even when our burdens are heavy.

July 4

Never Failing Love

"Charity [love] *never faileth . . . "* (I Cor. 13:8).

Broad statement, this— *"Love never faileth."*

First Paul gives a list of things that do fail, and they are the very things that we think would bring success. The list follows: eloquence of men and angels, the gift of prophecy, understanding all mysteries, having all knowledge, having all faith, giving all we have to feed the poor, and suffering martyrdom by fire. All of these can fail, but Paul almost seems to shout, *"Love never faileth."*

What Paul is saying is that love is long-suffering and kind, and that it is not envious. Love does not show off, is not rude, is not self-seeking, and it is slow to anger. Love does not think evil but loves the truth. Love is patient, trusting, hopeful. (See 1 Cor. 13:4-7). No wonder godly love does not fail.

The Bible tells us that we are to love God, love our neighbors, love the lost, and even love our enemies. Only God can give us such love. Paul tells us that *". . . the love of God is shed abroad in our hearts by the Holy Ghost which is given unto us"* (Rom. 5:5). This God-given love brings peace, joy and victory. *"Love never faileth."*

July 5

How Great Thou Art

"He telleth the number of the stars; he calleth them all by their names" (Psa. 147:4).

No man knows how many stars there are. Some have imagined there are as many stars as there are grains of sand on all the seashores in the world. The late Albert Einstein estimated that there must be at least ten octillion stars. That is the number 10 followed by 27 zeros.

God knows how many stars there are. He made everyone of them and named them. He calls them all by name.

Some years ago the largest dictionary in America was on display. It was said to contain 800,000 words. A library full of dictionaries that large could not contain the names of all the stars.

The God who knows the names of all the stars must know the name of every person who has ever lived. That means that He knows my name and your name. He knows where we live, and He loves us. Rejoice that we are His children and that He cares for us.

July 6

A Way to Live Longer

"MY son, forget not my law; but let thine heart keep my commandments: For length of days, and long life, and peace, shall they add to thee" (Prov. 3:1, 2).

Forty-two recent studies, involving 126 thousand people, have yielded overwhelming evidence that people who pray, read their Bibles, and go to church live longer on average than people who do not.

Without any studies we would know that is true. A person's life is better in every way when the blessings of God are upon it. Reading the Bible is uplifting. Prayer brings us in touch with God, and that brings peace to the heart. Trust in God relieves the pressure of worry. All of these contribute to a sense of well-being.

Serving God gives one purpose in life. There is always something we can do for others, and that gives us reason to want to go on living. We should claim God's promise of blessings upon our life, and make the most of every day He gives us.

July 7

The Power of Prayer

". . . The effectual fervent prayer of a righteous man availeth much" (James 5:16).

It is reported that one day Evan Roberts pointed to a rug with a big hole worn in it and asked, "Do you see that rug? There began the Welsh Revival. I wore that hole through with my knees as I prayed for the convicting power of the Holy Spirit upon the people. For five months before the revival began, I prayed agonizingly for the Holy Spirit. Each day I spent from 3 to 8 hours in prayer. I awoke each night at 1 o'clock and prayed."

Evan Roberts is only one of tens of millions who have prayed down the power of God and seen revivals come. The outstanding Jewish Evangelist, Hyman Appelman, was a man of prayer. One day when we had finished praying together, he turned to me and said, "Makes you feel good doesn't it?" Then he added, "I am never happy unless I am praying or preaching." He had outstanding revivals and won thousands to Christ.

Dr. Ford Porter, author of the tract, *God's Simple Plan of Salvation,* used to arise each morning at four o'clock, summer and winter, and go to his church to pray. He has gone to his reward, but his tract continues to be printed and mailed to the ends of the earth. God is still answering his prayers. You do not have to be a great leader in order to pray. Any child of God can pray.

July 8

Working Our Spiritual Garden

". . . work out your own salvation with fear and trembling" (Phil. 2:12).

We do not earn salvation by working for it. It is a gift of God. *"For by grace are ye saved through faith; and that not of yourselves: it is the gift of God: Not of works, lest any man should boast"* (Eph. 2:8, 9).

Since salvation is a gift why are we told to work out our salvation? We are to work out that which we already have. A gardener cannot work out his garden until he has one, but once he has a garden it will require plenty of work. For weeds will come up in it, and insects will be attracted to it. Just so, in the garden of the heart, Satan will sow his tares, and demons will seek to defeat us. For those reasons we are to work out our salvation.

We must constantly be on the watch for weeds of indifference, weeds of pride, weeds of jealousy, weeds of temptation, and on and on. We must eradicate these weeds by confessing and forsaking them. The Bible tells us that we can have perpetual cleansing. *"But if we walk in the light, as he is in the light, . . . the blood of Jesus Christ his Son cleanseth us from all sin"* (1 John 1:7). Continual cleansing will give us continual victory over temptation.

July 9

Laws in the Universe

"The soul that sinneth, it shall die . . ." (Ezek. 18:20).

Our Creator is a God of order. Everything in the universe operates by the laws He has set in order. There are physical laws, and there are spiritual laws. Violate either and you will pay a price.

There is the law of gravitation. It is a good law. Without it we would go flying off into space. But if we violate this law by falling and we may suffer injury or death. That would not be God's fault. It would simply be the law of cause and effect in operation.

God made electricity, and it operates by certain

laws. Electrical energy is good. It is hard to imagine life without its benefits, but if we violate its law by taking hold of a live wire we may suffer injury or death. Electricity is not to blame. Again, it is the cause and effect of violating the law by which it operates.

In the spiritual realm, the same is true. God's laws are good laws, but when we violate them we pay a price. The wages of sin is death. There is no reprieve when we fall or when we touch a live wire, but there is deliverance from the power of sin. The blood of Jesus saves from all sin. Those who receive Jesus as Saviour have eternal life. The body will die, but the soul will never die.

July 10

Mercy and Grace Are Available

"Seeing then that we have a great high priest, that is passed into the heavens, Jesus the Son of God . . . Let us therefore come boldly unto the throne of grace, that we may obtain mercy, and find grace to help in time of need" (Heb. 4:14, 16).

Jesus is our Saviour and our High Priest. As our High Priest He makes intercession for us at the right hand of God. For that reason Paul tells us that we can come boldly to the throne of grace and obtain mercy in the time of need.

Jesus understands our needs. He lived in the flesh and was tempted as we are tempted. He did not sin, but He understands when we are tempted. He knew loneliness, hunger, and fatigue. He suffered pain, sorrow, rejection, abuse and death. He understands all we have to go through and is touched with the feelings of our infirmities. When things go wrong, we should not become discouraged. We can go to the throne of grace in the time of need.

A man named Mel Trotter was an alcoholic and a bum. It has been said that when his baby died, neighbors made up money to buy shoes for its feet, but he stole the shoes and sold them to buy whiskey. After Mel Trotter was saved he became a great worker for the Lord. In his testimony he often said, "Jesus saved me from the gutter-most to the uttermost." Jesus will save anyone who will receive Him as Saviour, and He will give them victory over temptation.

July 11

Rejoice in Adversity

"Giving thanks always for all things unto God and the Father in the name of our Lord Jesus Christ" (Eph. 5:20).

"Always" and *"all things"* are important in this text. We should not let a day pass without giving thanks to God. We should give thanks for the good times that come our way and for the bad things as well.

We should never consider anything bad until God has finished with it. Often He turns bad things around and makes them blessings. Joseph must not have felt like thanking God when his brothers put him down in a well or when they sold him to slave traders who carried him to Egypt. He must not have felt like thanking God while he was in Potiphar's prison, but he had every reason to thank God after he was released from prison and made Prime Minister of Egypt.

The Apostle Paul suffered many trials, yet he had faith to write, *"And we know that all things work together for good to them that love God . . ."* (Rom. 8:28). Like Paul, we can give thanks in times of adversity, knowing that all things are working together for our good.

I once remarked to a psychologist that I was amazed that a blind man had become an outstanding musician. He replied, "It was most likely his handicap that caused him to invest the time and energy to develop his talent." Like this blind man, we can make our troubles stepping-stones to a place of achievement. It is not likely that Fanny Crosby would have written so many great hymns if she had not been blind. We need not desire trials, but we should thank God and use them when they come.

July 12

Walking in High Places

"How beautiful upon the mountains are the feet of him that bringeth good tidings . . . that publisheth salvation . . ." (Isa. 52:7).

Those who bring good tidings walk in high places. While walking the King's Highway, it is a beautiful experience to point others to the way that delivers from sin and leads to eternal life.

The way of salvation is clearly laid out in the Bible, but Satan blinds the minds of the unsaved. For that reason they need to have the clear message of the Gospel presented to them. Like the eunuch of Ethiopia, they cannot understand except someone guide them.

The Gospel should be lovingly presented, and prayer for the Holy Spirit to apply the Word and bring conviction is always needed. Often, after praying, only a word of encouragement is needed.

When a lost one receives Christ as Saviour, they should be encouraged to attend a Bible-preaching, soul-winning church, make an open confession, be baptized, and become a member of the church.

We are walking in high places on the mountain when we win the lost to Christ. There is no service that is higher.

July 13
We Have a Shield

"*. . . Fear not, Abram: I am thy shield, and thy exceeding great reward*" (Gen. 15:1).

In early times shields were made and used to protect men in battle. They were used to deflect darts, arrows, stones, swords, and spears. A soldier without a shield was easy prey to the enemy.

We often have to battle Satan and his forces. In Ephesians Paul describes this warfare and tells us how we are to be equipped for the battle. He tells us that we are to "*Put on the whole armour of God, that ye may be able to stand against the wiles of the devil,*" (Eph. 6:11). Then he adds, "*Above all, taking the shield of faith, wherewith ye shall be able to quench all the fiery darts of the wicked*" (verse 16).

It would be of small comfort if we only quench some of Satan's darts. Thank God that by faith we can quench all the fiery darts that Satan can hurl at us.

July 14

Light Conquers Darkness

"*He* (John the Baptist) *was not that Light, but was sent to bear witness of that Light. That was the true Light, which lighteth every man that cometh into the world*" (John 1:8, 9).

John the Baptist was a man sent from God, but

he was not the light of the world. He was only a witness of that Light. Jesus was and is the Light of the world.

Jesus came from the regions of light to this poor, sin-benighted world. Men loved darkness more than light, so they did not welcome Jesus when He came. *"He came unto His own, and his own received him not"* (John 1:11).

Jesus was born in a borrowed cradle, and during His sojourn on earth, He had no where to lay his head. He borrowed a boy's lunch to feed His followers. He rode into Jerusalem on a borrowed colt, and he borrowed an upper room for the Last Supper. He died on a cross that was furnished by the Roman government, and He was buried in a borrowed tomb.

Even though Jesus was rejected. He demonstrated the love of God. He made it clear that lost men must be born-again, and He told how that was possible. He extended an invitation to *"whosoever will,"* and He made it clear that He will never turn away a seeking soul.

July 15

Justification by Faith

"Therefore we conclude that a man is justified by faith without the deeds of the law" (Rom. 3:28).

Martin Luther described himself as an impeccable monk, but he knew he was not right with God. He wrote of himself: "I stood before God as a sinner, troubled in conscience." He knew that all his good works could not make him right with God. Then he learned from the book of Romans that God justifies by grace through faith. Of that discovery he wrote: "I felt myself to be reborn and to have gone through open doors into paradise."

Good works do not save. Receiving Jesus as Saviour does save. Jesus had no sin of His own, but He paid for our sins on the cross. When we receive Him as Saviour, our sin debt is canceled, and His righteousness is imputed to us. That means that credit is attributed to us.

Receiving Jesus as Saviour is the beginning of a journey of faith. The journey of faith will not end until we reach Heaven, but He will walk with us all the way. And, at the end of the journey, we will see Him face to face.

July 16
On Wings As Eagles

". . . they shall mount up with wings as eagles; they shall run, and not be weary . . ." (Isa. 40:31).

A man climbed in the Alps Mountains on foot for some hours. Finally he reached the clouds and passed through them. Above the clouds the sky was clear, and the sun was shining, but he soon heard thunder in the valley and knew that beneath the clouds a storm was raging.

As he watched the storm he saw something that looked like a golden ball emerge from the clouds. Fascinated, he watched the ball circle and rise until it was near enough for him to see that it was a golden eagle. The eagle had been caught in the storm and had spread its powerful wings, mounted upon the wind, and started its climb upward.

The eagle passed where he was standing and continued to climb. With its great wings it had left the storm behind, and it continued to climb until it was lost in the light of the sun.

When storms come our way, we can mount up on

wings of faith and soar above the clouds of darkness and into the glorious light of God's love. God has given us wings of faith, so we do not have to stay in the valley when storms come our way.

July 17
Helpful Commands

"Be ye angry, and sin not: let not the sun go down upon your wrath" (Eph. 4:26).

It is possible to become angry without sinning. We can control our anger so that no one will know we are angry. That means we will not say angry words. We can confess to God that we are angry and ask Him to forgive us, and we can forgive the one or the ones who have caused our anger.

Uncontrolled anger is sinful. It destroys peace of mind. It damages our relationship with others, and it can undermine our health.

It is sad that some Christians never learn to control their tempers. A lady is said to have remarked, "When I get mad it only lasts for a minute." So does an explosion, but it does great damage while it lasts.

We should never go to bed angry. Our text says, *". . . let not the sun go down upon your wrath."* We must forgive others, and we must become reconciled to those who are angry with us if possible. We cannot be right with God if we are not right with others.

July 18
Serving with Gladness

"Serve the LORD with gladness: come before his presence with singing" (Psa. 100:2).

Those who serve with gladness have a bright and cheerful countenance. This kind of serving brings honor to the Lord and joy and blessings to the server.

Those who serve with gladness do not dread serving. They do not complain or find fault. They do not serve to be applauded. They serve to honor the Lord and to be a blessing to others.

Those who serve the Lord with gladness can come into the Lord's presence with joy and singing. They are in position to commune with Him and worship Him. God blesses them and makes them a blessing. Their lives are like the dew of Mount Hermon. They bring refreshing to the lives of others, and they make the world a better place.

May God give us gladness of heart and make us a blessing to all we chance to meet.

July 19

Living Water

"He that believeth on me, as the scripture hath said, out of his belly (innermost being) *shall flow rivers of living water"* (John 7:38).

Jesus invites the unsaved to come to Him and drink the living water that He alone can give. He told the woman at the well, *"But whosoever drinketh of the water that I shall give him shall never thirst; but the water that I shall give him shall be in him a well of water springing up into everlasting life"* (John 4:14).

After we receive the water that Jesus gives, He expects us to become channels through which that water can flow to others. It is possible to become like a well that has almost gone dry. When that happens we become like an old pump of yesteryear. The pump had to be primed, and often it gave back less water than it took to prime it.

There must be an inflow before there can be an

outflow. We must stay close to the Lord for our cups to overflow. In that way we can have our own well of water springing up to everlasting life.

July 20

Our Sins Are Gone

". . . for thou hast cast all my sins behind thy back" (Isa. 38:17).

The Bible tells us that we have all sinned. *"For all have sinned, and come short of the glory of God"* (Rom. 3:23). How then can we be free of our sins? The Bible answers, *". . . the blood of Jesus Christ his Son cleanseth us from all sin"* (1 John 1:7).

Further, the Bible tells us that God gets rid of our sins. They are blotted out. *"I have blotted out, as a thick cloud, thy transgressions, and, as a cloud, thy sins . . ."* (Isa. 44:22). Our sins are buried in the sea. *". . . and thou wilt cast all their sins into the depths of the sea"* (Mic. 7:19). Our sins are removed far from us. *"As far as the east is from the west, so far hath he removed our transgressions from us"* (Psa. 103:12). How wonderful it is to know that our sins are gone.

After a revival service a man came to me with the following testimony: "I ran away from home and joined the navy before I was of age. While I was in the navy, I committed every sin in the book. My first Sunday back home after I got out of the navy, I went to church with my parents.

"The congregation sang the same old songs I had heard as a boy. The pastor preached the same kind of message, but something was different. I was tired of my sins, and I wanted to be saved. I trusted Jesus as my Saviour, and I walked out of the church feeling that I had just been born-again."

He had been born-again, and his sins were gone. That is true of every child of God. Praise God that our sins are gone.

July 21
The Unknown Path

"By faith Abraham . . .went out, not knowing whither he went" (Heb. 11:8).

Abraham was called to go to a land he had never seen. There were no road maps to show him the way, but in Genesis 12:1 God told him that He would show him the land. That meant that God would guide him to the land.

We too are going to a Land we have never seen, but we have a road map. The Bible tells us how to get on the road that leads to that Land, and it tells us how to conduct ourselves on the way. Even so, we are traveling through strange territory, and there are times when we have to walk by faith.

On the journey to our Promised Land, we will have to pass through unexpected valleys and climb treacherous mountains. There will be times of darkness, and times of unexpected trials. There will be disappointments, times of sorrow, and times of suffering.

The Bible does not tell us how to avoid these, but it does tell us how we can find strength for the journey. Our heavenly Father has promised never to leave us. Even when we can not feel His presence, He is only a prayer away. Rest assured that He will be with us until we reach the city of God.

July 22
Rest For the Soul

"Take my yoke upon you, and learn of me; for I

am meek and lowly in heart: and ye shall find rest unto your souls" (Matt. 11:29).

It is possible to be tired beyond reason. Even after a good night's sleep we often feel tired. We are supposed to get rested on a vacation, but we often return from a vacation more tired than we were when we left home.

There is more than one cause for being tired. We can be tired in body. That can be caused by hours of physical activity or by insufficient sleep. The energy that keeps us going is depleted, so we have to rest and sleep to recharge our batteries.

Another kind of tiredness is mental tiredness. That is caused by mental activity, pressure, worry, sorrow, or a combination of all of these. This condition may be relieved when we stop worrying, learn to work relaxed, take frequent breaks, and take time off from work.

A third kind of tiredness is soul tiredness. This can be caused by a guilty conscious, pent-up anger, grudge holding or other negative emotions. Our text tells us to take on the Lord's yoke (get saved) and learn of Him, and we will find rest for our souls. He will cleanse us from all sin, enable us to trust in Him and not worry, for He will be our constant guide and companion.

July 23
The Easy Yoke

"For my yoke is easy, and my burden is light" (Matt. 11:30).

A yoke is a crossbar with two U-shaped pieces that encircle the necks of a pair of oxen so they can share the burden they are called upon to bear.

In my boyhood my father had two work mules. One was named Ol' Jack, and the other was named Ol' Kit. Ol' Jack was much larger and much stronger than Ol' Kit, but my father hitched them both to the same load. He equalized the load for the two mules by using a doubletree with a long end and a short end. The small mule was hitched to the long end, and the large mule was hitched to the short end. That way the large mule pulled most of the load. Just so, when we are yoked up with Jesus, He carries most of the load, and that makes our burden light.

July 24
Be Steadfast

"But none of these things move me . . ." (Acts 20:24).

The Apostle Paul had gone through more than his share of trials, and the Holy Spirit had told him that bonds and afflictions would continue to be his lot. Now he was going to Jerusalem, not knowing what trials would await him there. The memory of past trials and the expectation of future trials were upon him, yet he exults, *"None of these things move me."*

Knowing the trials Paul had experienced, and the pressure of other trials he was facing, gives added emphasis to his admonition, *"Therefore, my beloved brethren, be ye stedfast, unmoveable, always abounding in the work of the Lord . . . "* (1 Cor. 15:58).

Someone has said, "The measure of a man's character is what it takes to stop him." Paul leaves no room for us to stop serving the Lord. Always we must abound in the work of the Lord. We should do our best for Him today and in all of our future days of our life.

July 25
Victory over Temptation

". . . but God is faithful, who will not suffer you to be tempted above that ye are able; but will with the temptation also make a way to escape . . ." (1 Cor. 10:13).

We are all subject to temptation. Satan tempted angels and caused them to fall. He tempted Jesus, and he certainly will tempt us. God has not promised that we will not be tempted, but He has promised to give us victory over temptation. When Satan fences us in, God will make a way for us to escape.

Little eight year-old Mary, made a profession of faith. Because of her tender age, the pastor wanted to make sure that she understood what she was doing. "Mary, if the devil knocks on your heart's door and tempts you to do something wrong, what will you do?" he asked.

"I'll ask Jesus to go to the door, and the devil will go away," she answered.

When God makes a way for us to escape temptation, we should take advantage of it. That often means removing ourselves from the presence of temptation. When that is true we should flee from the presence of temptation as Joseph fled from Potiphar's wife when she tempted him to sin.

July 26
Bottled Prayers

". . . Thy prayers . . . are come up for a memorial before God" (Acts 10:4).

A marvelous thought—volumes of meaning here. Cornelius prayed to God always. He had been praying for a time, perhaps years, when an angel appeared and told him that his prayers had come up for a memorial before God. It seems that his years of prayers had accumulated before the throne of God, and they suddenly broke in blessings upon him.

In Revelation 5:8 we read of golden vials full of odors, which are the prayers of saints, and in Revelation 8:3 we read of an angel offering incense with the prayers of saints upon a golden altar before the throne of God.

It appears that when God does not answer our prayers at once, they are stored to be answered at a later time. Often the answer to a prayer comes weeks or years after it is offered. The answer may even come after we are in Heaven. Our loved ones in glory must rejoice when prayers they offered while they were on earth are answered. The very thought should encourage us to pray.

July 27
Giving Our Best

"So, as much as in me is, I am ready to preach the gospel to you that are at Rome also" (Rom. 1:15).

Paul is saying, I am ready to preach the Gospel with all my strength, energy, ability, and power. We are not all preachers, but we can all give our best in the service of God. We should never be satisfied to give less than our best.

Years ago, I asked a layman in Detroit why the church he attended was so successful in reaching the lost for Christ. His answer contains the greatest one-line sermon I have ever heard. An approximate quote follows.

"People in my church meet on week nights to pray, plan, and go witnessing to people in their homes. Our people are sold out to God." Now here is the one line sermon. "Take myself for example, I work for the Ford Motor Company to pay my expenses, but my business is serving God." It would be wonderful if every Christian could honestly say, "My business is serving God."

July 28
God Delights to Bless His Children
". . . Let the LORD be magnified, which hath pleasure in the prosperity of his servant" (Psa. 35:27).

The Bible has much to say about prosperity. In the first Psalm it is written of the godly man, *". . . whatsoever he doeth shall prosper."* In Psalms 37:25 David wrote, *". . . yet have I not seen the righteous forsaken, nor his seed begging bread."* Paul wrote, *"But my God shall supply all your need according to his riches in glory by Christ Jesus"* (Phil. 4:19).

God especially blesses those who give generously of their money. Jesus said, *"Give, and it shall be given unto you; good measure, pressed down, and shaken together, and running over . . . For with the same measure that ye mete withal it shall be measured to you again"* (Luke 6:38).

The only time in the Bible that God said, *"prove me."* was with reference to tithing (Mal. 3:10). Solomon gives this bit of wisdom in Proverbs. *"Honour the LORD with thy substance, and with the firstfruits of thine increase: So shall thy barns be filled with plenty . . ."* (Prov. 3:9, 10).

Those who are generous in their giving are in position to be blessed of God.

July 29
The Danger of Fear
"For the thing which I greatly feared is come upon me . . ." (Job 3:25).

God said that Job was a good man, but his thinking was wrong. His mind was filled with fear, and fear and faith cannot stay in the heart at the same time. One or the other will triumph. Job was afraid that his sons and daughters had sinned and would be punished. So he offered burnt offerings for them. He hoped his religious act would keep them from being punished. Still he was afraid, and his fear opened the door for all kinds of trouble to come upon him.

After he had lost his possessions, his children, his health, the respect of his wife, and the esteem of his friends, he cried, *"For the thing which I greatly feared is come upon me . . ."* (Job 3:25).

It was only after Job forgot his troubles and started praying for his friends that God blessed him. *"And the Lord turned the captivity of Job, when he prayed for his friends . . ."* (Job 42:10). We should get our minds and hearts set upon God. In that way we can conquer our fears and live victoriously.

July 30

When Afraid, Trust in God

"What time I am afraid, I will trust in thee" (Psa. 56:3).

When David wrote our text, he had enough trouble to cause him to be constantly afraid, so he must have been constantly trusting in the Lord. The more trouble we have, the more we should trust in the Lord.

Trials can serve a purpose. They can build faith, but they can also breed defeat. It depends on which way one is looking. Looking up instead of down can help. Looking unto Jesus instead of looking at conditions can build faith. And looking into the Word of God will build faith. Paul wrote, *"So then faith*

cometh by hearing, and hearing by the word of God"
(Rom. 10:17).

Our faith needs exercise to grow strong. We
should use it often.

July 31

God's Word Blesses

*". . . It is written, That man shall not live by bread
alone, but by every word of God"* (Luke 4:4).

The Word of God is bread for those who are spiritually hungry. It is a tower of strength to those who
are weak. It is a faith builder to those whose faith is
weak. It is a light to those who are passing through a
dark valley. It is a lighthouse to those who are in the
troubled sea of life. It is a guiding star when the compass fails, and it is a steadfast anchor when the storm
rages.

We need spiritual food just as we need physical
food. Reading the Word of God will build spiritual
strength. Hiding the Word of God in our hearts will
help us overcome temptation (Psa. 119:11).

The Word of God is spiritually discerned (1 Cor.
2:14). We should read and study it reverently and
prayerfully. The Holy Spirit is our teacher, and He
will open our minds to understand truths that have
been obscure to us. The Word of God is a gold mine.
We should dig for nuggets of truth and grow strong
in the Lord.

Devotions for August

August 1
Blessed Winds

"Awake, O north wind; and come, thou south; blow upon my garden, that the spices thereof may flow out . . ." (Song of Sol. 4:16).

The maiden in the Song of Solomon represents the church, and the man represents the heavenly Bridegroom. Her prayer for the north wind and the south wind to blow upon her garden is a prayer for the garden of her heart to be prepared for the coming of the Bridegroom.

It is not the stillness but the blowing of the winds that brings forth the fragrance of the spices. The blowing of the winds also contributes to the growth of the trees. In like manner the winds of trial that blow upon us contribute to our spiritual growth. Peter wrote, *"That the trial of your faith, being much more precious than of gold that perisheth . . . might be found unto praise and honour and glory at the appearing of Jesus Christ"* (1 Pet. 1:7).

There must be sweetness in the heart for the blowing winds to bring forth sweetness. The wind blowing upon a thistle will never bring forth the fragrance of a spice tree. To be ready for the coming of the Bridegroom, our hearts must be surrendered to Him and we must be filled with His Spirit.

August 2

Growing in the Lord

". . . add to your faith . . ." (2 Pet. 1:5).

Peter writes of receiving the divine nature through faith, then tells us to add to our faith virtue, knowledge, temperance, patience, godliness, brotherly kindness, and love. This means that we are to grow in the Lord. A child that does not grow is an unhealthy child. A Christian who does not grow is an unhealthy Christian.

Peter adds, *"For if these things be in you, and abound, they make you that ye shall neither be barren nor unfruitful . . ."* (Verse 8).

The story is told of a man who attended church regularly, always sat in the same place, and always left after the service without participating in any way. One day someone asked, "Why do you always just sit and do nothing?" He replied, "When I joined the church, someone said, 'Sit down over there' and I did."

Someone has well said, "We should stand on the promises, not simply sit on the premises." We are not saved to sit. We are saved to grow in the Lord and to be useful in His service.

August 3

Getting Prayers Answered

"And whatsoever we ask, we receive of him, because we keep his commandments, and do those things that are pleasing in his sight" (1 John 3:22).

Prayers are meant to be answered. We are serving a prayer hearing and a prayer answering God. In place after place the Bible gives us keys for getting our prayers answered. Our text for today contains three of these keys. 1. We must be saved. 2. We must be obedient. 3. We must please the Lord.

Many good Christians have trouble with the last of these. Though they are in the place God has appointed for them, the devil fills their minds with doubt. We must learn to be content and to serve God where we are. If God has other plans for our lives, in time He will reveal them. Just now, if our prayers are to be answered, we are to live right and serve the Lord to the best of our ability. That includes doings things just to please Him.

August 4

Conquering Fear

"Fear thou not; for I am with thee . . ." (Isa. 41:10).

What a wonderful promise we have here. God is with us. That should give us assurance, yet there are those who live in fear. They fear when there is no cause for fear. They allow Satan to make them fear that something terrible is going to happen. Without realizing the source of their fear, they begin to worry, and that destroys their peace of mind and their sense of well-being. And that hinders their service for the Lord.

We should trust and not be afraid. God plainly says, *"Fear thou not."* In the next phrase, He tells us that He is with us. God's promise is in the present tense. He is with us now, and, no matter what happens, He will continue to be with us in the future.

That does not mean that we will never have any trouble, but it does mean that God will be with us and will go with us through our troubles. In Isaiah 43:2 God promises to be with us when we pass through the waters and walk through the fire. So we should put our fears aside and walk with God by faith. In that way we can have continual victory.

August 5
Be Prosperous and Happy

"For thou shall eat the labour of thine hands: happy shalt thou be, and it shall be well with thee" (Psa. 128:2).

The promises of this verse are conditional. The word *"For"* harks back to verse one, which says, *"BLESSED is every one that feareth the LORD; that walketh in his ways."* To enjoy the prosperity and happiness promised in our text, we must be saved, and we must be walking in God's will.

God loves His children and wants to bless them. Only those who fear Him enough to receive Jesus as their Saviour are His children, and only those who are walking in His will can claim the promises of our text.

Not every saved person is completely surrendered to God. One treasured desire or one worldly pursuit stands in their way. We should realize that the treasured desire or worldly pursuit is far too costly. The thing that keeps us from complete surrender is only dust and ashes when compared to blessings that are lost because we are not in the center of God's will. God has a perfect will for our life. We should find IIis will and walk in it.

August 6
Walk in Glory

"And the glory which thou gavest me I have given them; that they may be one, even as we are one" (John 17:22).

This text is taken from the prayer Jesus prayed for His disciples. The words glory and glorify are used five times in that prayer. The late A. B. Simpson wrote, "The word glory is very difficult to translate, define, and explain."

Glory has to do with God. He is a glorious being, and Heaven is a glorious place. *"THE heavens declare the glory of God. . ."* (Psa. 19:1). The angels sing of His glory. The seraphims declare, *"The whole earth is full of His glory"* (Isa. 6:3).

Jesus had glory with the Father before the world was (John 17:5), yet He speaks of the glory God had given Him. Perhaps that was the glory He was given in this world.

How marvelous that we are also given glory. To be saved is glorious. To walk with God is glorious. To pray and get answers to our prayers is glorious. To have reasons for living is glorious, and when we leave this world, "It will be only glory for eternity."

August 7

Let Us Be Faithful

"And let us not be weary in well doing: for in due season we shall reap, if we faint not" (Gal. 6:9).

We are not to grow weary in doing good, and we are not to faint. To faint means to give up. If we remain faithful we are promised that we will reap in due season.

Those who raise gardens realize that there are seasons. There is the season of cultivation, the season of planting, the season of growth, and the season of harvest. The season is not the same for all plants, but they all have a season. We do not reap by giving up. Continuing to work will bring a harvest in due time.

The same is true in the spiritual realm. We are to

continue to do well even when we are discouraged.

The well doing in our text deals with doing good to other Christians. In the next verse we read, *"As we have therefore opportunity, let us do good unto all men, especially unto them who are of the household of faith."*

It is possible to become so busy doing our job in our church that we forget to do good to others. When I first became a pastor, as a very young preacher, an older lady gave me some sage advice. Said she, "You have to win the love and respect of your people before you can lead them." There is no better way to win the love and respect of people than by living a godly life and doing good to them.

Doing good to the unsaved may help win them to Christ. Doing good to the saved may help them in a time of need. We should strive to be a blessing instead of trying to get a blessing. We are promised a harvest if we continue to do good to others.

August 8
Trusting When Things Go Bad

"And it came to pass after a while, that the brook dried up, because there had been no rain in the land" (1 Kings 17:7).

Elijah was in the will of God, but after a while things started to look bad for him. God had sent him to tell King Ahab that there would be no rain or dew for some years. In Luke 4:25 we read that the drought lasted three and one-half years.

God told Elijah to hide by the brook Cherith during the drought. He could drink from the brook, and ravens would bring him bread and meat, morning and evening.

It must have been trying to Elijah's faith when

the brook started going dry, but he stayed where God had placed him. The brook receded day after day, but Elijah stayed on. At last, the brook was completely dry. God had other provisions for Elijah, but he did not move from where God had placed him until God told him to move.

There are times when we need faith to stay where God has placed us, even when things look bad. Faith does not depend upon conditions; it depends upon the promises of God.

August 9

Others

"Be kindly affectioned one to another with brotherly love; in honour preferring one another" (Rom. 12:10).

It is natural for us to look out for ourselves and to let others fend for themselves, but as Christians we should honor and serve others.

Years ago, Dr. John Hamilton practiced medicine in a small town in Pennsylvania. He became popular with the well-to-do people and made a lot of money, but drinking ruined his life and drove him from his practice. He left town in disgrace.

Five years later he returned and opened an upstairs office in the poor part of town. A painted sign, with a hand pointing upward, read, "Dr. John Hamilton, Office Upstairs."

His first patient was a little boy named Jimmy Kelley. He straightened Jimmy's twisted legs so he could walk. The poor people came to love Dr. Hamilton so much that when he died, they unhitched the horses from the hearse and pulled it to the graveside themselves.

There was no stone for the grave, so Jimmy Kelley

ran to the doctor's office and got his sign. They placed it on the grave with the hand pointing upward and the words reading, "Dr. John Hamilton, Office Upstairs."

Dr. Hamilton had served others, and others honored him after he had gone to his reward. His example is a challenge for us to serve others also.

August 10

Always Rejoicing

"As sorrowful, yet alway rejoicing . . ." (2 Cor. 6:10).

Contrary terms! Sorrowful, yet rejoicing? That was the way Paul expressed it and the way he lived. He had learned that God can put joy in the heart that nothing can take away. The roll call (in the preceding verses) of the sufferings he and his co-laborers were going through was enough to drive them all into the dungeon of depression. Yet Paul writes that they were always rejoicing. Nothing could rob them of their joy.

On another occasion Paul and Silas were arrested, beaten, put in stocks, and thrown into the Philippian jail, but they still had victory. At midnight they sang praises to God so loud that the other prisoners heard them. Their joy was unquenchable.

Paul's letter to the Philippians was written from a damp, cold, vermin-infested prison. Yet in this brief letter of 4 chapters, he used the words joy, rejoice, rejoiced and rejoicing, 16 times. His joy did not depend upon conditions.

Joy is the birthright of every Christian. Jesus said, *"These things have I spoken unto you, that my joy might remain in you, and that your joy might be full"* (John 15:11).

We Christians do not have to live in gloom and despair. Even when it is dark we can walk in the joy of the Lord.

August 11
Keeping the Faith

"... *I have kept the faith*" (2 Tim. 4:7).

Paul had gone through every trial Satan had put in his way, and he could still declare, *"I have kept the faith."* The following verse from an old song would probably have been his favorite if it had been written in his day.

> Through many dangers, toils, and snares
> I have already come.
> 'Tis grace hath brought me safe thus far,
> And grace will lead me home.

Paul was nearing the end, and, surveying his life from that vantage point, he rejoiced in three things. He had fought a good fight, he had finished the course, and he had kept the faith. In the end he lost his head, but he never lost his faith. Even though they were going to cut off his head, he was looking forward to wearing a crown of righteousness (verse 8). He knew that his head would be in place on his resurrected body. His faith did not fail even when the time drew near for him to be beheaded.

As God was with Paul, He can be with us, and He can give us faith to face ever trial that comes our way.

August 12
Water to Share

"... *but the water that I shall give him shall be in him a well of water springing up into everlasting life*" (John 4:14).

When the Samaritan woman came to Jacob's Well to draw water, Jesus used the occasion to tell her about the water of life. He told her that she could have a well of water in her heart that would never run dry. It would be an artesian well, springing up and overflowing. We get the picture of a well that would overflow and bring others in contact with everlasting life.

It is tragic that many believers allow some trivial thing to clog the well of water in their hearts and stop it from flowing. A clogged well is a stagnant well, and it cannot bring blessings to others.

The Jordan River flows into the Sea of Galilee, then through it and down the valley. The same river flows into the Dead Sea, but it does not flow out of it. Because the Sea of Galilee gives forth as much as it receives, it is a body of living water. The Dead Sea is dead because it receives, but it does not give. If we are to remain spiritually alive, we must allow God's blessing to flow through us and bless the lives of others.

August 13
Praying for Our Needs

"Give us this day our daily bread" (Matt. 6:11).

In the Lord's model prayer we are taught to pray for the honor of the Father's name, and for His will to be done on earth before we pray for bread. We can pray for things we need, but we should worship God first.

There are many examples of those who have received things they needed in answer to prayer. One example follows. In the early part of the 19th century, a sea captain told of an encounter with a preacher named George Mueller that changed his life. The captain had been on the bridge of his fog-bound ship, off the coast of Newfoundland for twenty-four hours when Mueller came to him and told him that he had to be in Quebec to preach on Saturday.

"That will not be possible," the captain told him.

"Then, I'll find another way to get there," Mueller said. "I have not missed an appointment in fifty-seven years."

The captain was sure Mueller had come out of some insane asylum when he suggested that they go to the chart room and pray. When they reached the chart room Mueller prayed a simple prayer then asked the captain not to pray, telling him that God had already answered his prayer.

When the captain looked out the fog was gone.

God does answer prayers for daily needs. When we pray and the answer does not come, we should try to discover why. The reason may be that our motive is wrong. James tells us, *"Ye ask, and receive not, because ye ask amiss, that ye may consume it upon your lusts"* (James 4:3).

Jonathan Edwards, an outstanding preacher in the 18th century, wrote: "The one concern of the devil is to keep the saints from prayer. He fears nothing from prayerless studies, prayerless work, and prayerless religion. He laughs at our toil, mocks at our wisdom, but trembles when we pray."

August 14
Beginning Again

"And he went on his journeys from the south, even to Bethel . . . Unto the place of the altar, which he had made there at the first . . ." (Gen. 13:3, 4).

Sometimes we have to go backward in order to go forward. Abram left Bethel and went to Egypt in a time of famine. Bethel means the house of God.

Egypt is a type of the world. Pharaoh is a type of the devil. In other words, Abram allowed trouble to cause him to backslide.

Abram ran into trouble as backsliders always do. Pharaoh took his wife from him, but when he learned that she was Abram's wife, he gave her back to him and expelled them from his country. It must have been a stormy scene when Pharaoh drove them out of Egypt.

At once Abram started back to where he had been before he backslid. He went back to Bethel, the house of God, and back to the altar he had built there. He had learned his lesson. We never read of him getting out of God's will again.

All too often good people, drop out of church and go back to the world because of trial or because of some misunderstanding. Like Abram they run into trouble. The only way out of their problem is for them to go back to the house of God and back to the altar of repentance.

August 15

Blessed Stillness

"Be still, and know that I am God . . ." (Psa. 46:10).

In this day many people are addicted to noise. The usual background noise is not enough for them, so they are never satisfied without a radio, a TV, or a music player going full blast. There are even those who want the volume loud enough to make them vibrate. If they are in an automobile, they want the volume of whatever they are playing to be loud enough to be heard half a block away. It is little wonder that God says, *"Be still, and know that I am God."*

We all need some quiet time alone so God can

communicate with us. It is tragic that some people never realize that they need God until some tragedy overtakes them. When tragedy shuts them off from the usual noise they often realize that God is trying to get their attention.

A man who was suddenly diagnosed with a life-threatening illness said, "God was trying to get my attention, and I listened." That experience changed his life. It is far better to make quiet times so we can hear from God, than it is to wait until He claims our attention through some trial or even some tragedy.

August 16
Blessed Dwelling Place

"They that dwell under his shadow shall return; they shall revive as the corn, and grow as the vine . . ." (Hos. 14:7).

It is not enough to make an occasional courtesy call on the Lord, nor is it enough to only visit Him when we need something.

We can always tell when a deadbeat is attempting to take advantage of us. He will begin by telling us how wonderful he thinks we are. He will tell how much he appreciates us. Then he will get around to asking for money or for some other favor. We certainly do not want to use the Lord in that way. He knows when we're not sincere. We should never try to use God just to get something we want. Instead, we should dwell under His shadow. That is where the blessings are located.

The corn and the vine suffer in times of drought, but they revive when God sends rain upon them. We all go through dry seasons, and we wonder why God is not blessing us, or why He is not answering our prayers. In such times we should continue to dwell under the shadow of our Lord, knowing that in due time His blessings will come.

August 17
We Have a Shelter

"For thou hast been a shelter for me, and a strong tower from the enemy" (Psa. 61:3).

Years ago, a visiting preacher came to preach one Sunday night in the village church where I was pastoring. Just after his opening remarks, a sudden deluge of rain started pouring on the tin roof of the church. The roar of the rain was so loud no one could hear the preacher, so he paused and waited for the storm to pass. When the storm finally ended he told the following story.

As a small boy, he was caught in a hailstorm one day when he was playing near a farm wagon. To escape the storm, he ran under the wagon and climbed on the coupling pole. When the storm ended, he came from his hiding place. There was plenty of hail in the wagon bed, but none of it had reached him. He then made the point that God is our shelter in the time of storm. We need God at all times. We should not wait for a storm to drive us to Him, but it is great to know that He is our shelter when storms come.

It is good to know that God is our shelter, and we shelter beneath His mighty arms when the storms of life come. Storms should never drive us away from God. They should drive us closer to God. He is our shelter and our strong tower.

August 18
God Is Our Guide

"For thou art my rock and my fortress; therefore for thy name's sake lead me, and guide me" (Psa. 31:3).

In our verse for today the Psalmist prays, *". . . lead me and guide me."* That should be our prayer also. We are not to choose our way then ask God to bless us. Instead we are to let Him lead us to the way of His choosing. There is joy and blessings in God's perfect will that we can find nowhere else. We should seek to know His perfect will, and when we find it we should walk in it.

God's Guidance

Morning knocks upon my door,
    And the shadows flee away.
Ere my feet have touched the floor,
    I feel the need to pray.

This day is new and strange to me.
    Never before have I passed this way.
There may be pitfalls I will not see,
    So I need God's guidance in the way.

—Anonymous

August 19

The High Rock

". . . when my heart is overwhelmed: lead me to the rock that is higher than I" (Psa. 61:2).

To be overwhelmed is to be submerged or engulfed. It is to be like a ship that is overwhelmed by titanic waves in a terrific storm. We can be overwhelmed when something is too much for us to handle. When that happens we should appeal to the Lord, our rock of deliverance.

We can usually handle our little problems, but we sometimes encounter problems that we cannot handle. That is when we need God's help. There are no problems that He cannot handle. As believers, we are His children, and He cares for us. That is why the Bible tells us to cast our care upon Him (1 Pet. 5:7).

There is an old song that says, "Take your burden to the Lord and leave it there." We are not supposed to take our burdens to the Lord then keep on carrying them. We should take our burdens to the Lord and let Him handle them. That way we can stop worrying and start trusting.

August 20
Joyful Worship

". . . I had gone with the multitude, I went with them to the house of God, with the voice of joy and praise . . ." (Psa. 42:4).

Here we have a beautiful picture. A multitude of people were going to the house of God to worship, and the writer of this Psalm went with them. They went to worship with joy and praise. This should be so with us every time we go to church.

Churches should be houses of praise and worship, but often they are places of discouragement. Discouraged pastors often face discouraged congregations and preach discouraging sermons. Neither the pastor or the congregation are helped. They often leave the church more discouraged than they were when they came.

God is not a God of failure. He is a God of success. True faith, coupled with prayer, worship, and praise can drive out the dismal fog of discouragement and replace it with the sunlight of victory.

August 21
Reasons for Praising God

"BLESS the LORD, O my soul: and all that is within me, bless his holy name" (Psa. 103:1).

One of the meanings of the word bless is to honor. Certainly we should honor and praise the name of our heavenly Father.

Someone has pointed out that this verse is in the very center of the Bible, and well it should be. Nothing is more central to our faith than honoring and praising God.

Verse 2 of this psalm tells us that we should bless the Lord for all His benefits. Verses 3, 4, and 5 list some of the benefits of serving the Lord. These verses follow. *"Who forgiveth all thine iniquities; who healeth all thy diseases; Who redeemeth thy life from destruction; who crowneth thee with lovingkindness and tender mercies; Who satisfieth thy mouth with good things; so that thy youth is renewed like the eagle's."*

The last benefit mentioned does not mean that we will become sixteen instead of sixty. It does mean that we can be younger than our years. Research has shown that people who attend church and pray tend to live longer and have better health than those who do not. Besides that, in Heaven we will be young forever.

August 22

Help When Needed

"Fear thou not; for I am with thee: be not disamayed; for I am thy God: I will strengthen thee; yea, I will help thee; yea, I will uphold thee . . ." (Isa. 41:10).

Here is a promise that God will give us the help we need in time of trouble. When our burdens are more than we can bear, He will give us added strength. When our trials are more than we can handle, God promises to help us. When our trials pile up like ocean waves and threaten to overwhelm us, God promises to uphold us. When our trials are too great for us, God will come to our rescue.

Someone has pointed out that if we could view our footprints in the sands of time, in some places there would be two sets of prints. In other places there would only be one set of prints. The two sets of prints were made when Jesus walked beside us. The single set of prints were made when He carried us. We should take comfort that God has promised, ". . . as *thy days, so shall thy strength be"* (Deut. 33:25).

August 23
Blessed Fellowship

"We took sweet counsel together, and walked unto the house of God in company" (Psa. 55:14).

God's people should attend church regularly. God says in His Word, *"Not forsaking the assembling of ourselves together, as the manner of some is . . ."* (Heb. 10:25). Attending church affords us a place to find fellowship, to learn, to grow, to worship, and to serve.

There is no fellowship so sweet as the fellowship of God's people. Like those of old, we can take sweet counsel together, and we will be better for it.

How beautiful it is to see God's people walking into the house of God in company. It is beautiful to see families seated together, singing together, worshiping together, and listening together to the preaching of God's Word.

There are many reasons for attending church. We will be better Christians when we attend church regularly. Our homes will be better when we attend church as families. America will be better when more people attend church. America is coarsened and made worse by the people who do not attend church.

August 24

Eternal Praise

*"PRAISE ye the LORD. Praise ye the LORD from
the heavens: praise him in the heights. Praise ye him,
all his angels: praise ye him, all his hosts. Praise ye
him, sun and moon: praise him, all ye stars of light.
Praise him, ye heavens of heavens, and ye waters
that be above the heavens. Let them praise the name
of the LORD: for he commanded, and they were created"* (Psa. 148:1-5).

The created universe attests the glory of our God.
*"THE heavens declare the glory of God; and the fir-
mament sheweth his handywork"* (Psa. 19:1).

There will come a time when eternal morning will
dawn. There will be no more night. All rebellion will
be banished from the Heaven of heavens, and a time
of universal praise will begin. The sun and moon and
blazing stars will praise the Lord. All the angels and
all the heavenly hosts will praise Him forever.

In this sinful world only saved people praise the
Lord. We praise Him because we love Him, and we
praise Him that others may know that we are His
children. Our praise is a testimony while we live, and
the memory of our praise will be a testimony after
we are gone. Then in Heaven, we will praise Him
forever.

August 25

Dealing with Infirmities

*". . . Most gladly therefore will I rather glory in
my infirmities, that the power of Christ may rest upon
me"* (2 Cor. 12:9).

Even the great Apostle Paul had some infirmities. One of them could have been his thorn in the flesh. He rejoiced in his infirmities because they made him more dependent upon the power of Christ. He even wrote, *"Therefore I take pleasure in infirmities . . . for when I am weak, then am I strong"* (2 Cor. 12:10).

Paul could have pouted. Or he could have become despondent. If he had done either his ministry would have suffered, for he would have lost the power of God upon his life. Paul made an intelligent decision, and there is no reason to believe that it was a reluctant decision. Concerning his decision he wrote that he would glory in his infirmities that God's power might rest upon him.

In spite of the pain, Paul continued to give his best in God's service. To this day his thorn in the flesh is an example to those who suffer.

Paul's experience helps us to understand, that when God does not give us what we pray for, it does not mean that He has not answered our prayer. God often gives us something better than what we pray for. Added grace can be the answer.

August 26

Our Great High Priest

"For we have not an high priest which cannot be touched with the feeling of our infirmities; but was in all points tempted like as we are, yet without sin" (Heb. 4:15).

Jesus lived in this world as a man. As our high priest He knows all about our troubles and our trials. He understands when we are weak, and He invites us to come to Him in our times of need.

There are four great truths in our text for today: 1. Jesus is our high priest. 2. He is touched by our weaknesses. 3. He was tempted as we are tempted. 4. He conquered every temptation known to man.

Jesus knows when we are tempted. He knew that Peter was going to be tried by Satan before Peter knew it, and He told Peter that He had already prayed that his faith would not fail. As our high priest Jesus makes intercession for us. We will never know in this life how many times we have been delivered from trials and temptations in answer to the prayers our Lord has offered for us. Thank God that Jesus is our high priest at God's right hand.

August 27

The Still Small Voice

"... and after the fire a still small voice" (1 Kings 19:12).

Elijah had gone through great trials—three and one half years of drought, the contest with the prophets of Baal, the flight from the wrath of Queen Jezebel, weariness and loneliness beneath the juniper tree, and, finally, despondency. He even prayed to die. Instead of taking the life of the defeated prophet as he had prayed, God sent an angel to feed him. It must have been in a voice of sympathy that God said to him, *"... the journey is too great for thee"* (verse 7).

Elijah left the juniper tree and went to Horeb, the mount of God. There God demonstrated His power in a wind, in an earthquake, and in a fire. After that God spoke to him in a still small voice.

God often speaks to us in a still small voice today. The still small voice is felt, not heard. It may begin as a gentle impression in the heart. In time it can become an imperative command.

However the still small voice is perceived, we should heed it. John wrote to each of the seven churches in the Revelation, *"He that hath an ear, let him hear what the Spirit saith unto the churches"* (Rev. 3:22).

August 28

How to Stop Worrying

"Be careful for nothing (don't worry about anything)*; but in every thing by prayer and supplication with thanksgiving let your requests be made known unto God"* (Phil. 4:6).

Some years ago I heard a Christian lawyer give the following testimony. When he first started in his practice he and his family lived on a farm, and he was raising corn to help pay expenses. His practice was slow, and he could hardly sleep at night for worrying.

One night he dreamed that his children were all down with typhoid fever, and his wife had lost her mind. He was spending all his time taking care of them. Then he looked out the window and saw the neighbor's cows in his cornfield devouring his corn. On his way out to drive the cows out of the corn, he saw a thief in the house stealing all their valuables. He awoke and realized he had been dreaming. He felt condemned that he had been worrying over a small problem, and he promised the Lord that he would stop worrying.

Our verse for today tells us not to worry but to pray about everything. Prayer is the antidote for worry. We should make it a habit to let our requests be known to God in prayer.

August 29

Wait to Know the Will of God

". . . Then I knew that this was the word of the LORD" (Jer. 32:8).

Jeremiah had been imprisoned by King Zedekiah because the king did not like what he had prophesied. While he was in prison God told him that his uncle's son would come to him and ask him to buy his field. It was only after that prophecy was fulfilled that Jeremiah said, *". . . I knew that this was the word of the LORD."*

When we are not sure how the Lord is leading, it is wise to wait until circumstances show us how He is leading. The confirmation of how God is leading may not come at once. It may not come for some time. When it does not come at once, we should wait on the Lord.

Sometimes the confirmation will come in the form of a series of events that fit together like the pieces of a jigsaw puzzle. The pieces fit together so perfectly that we know that only God could have arranged it. When that happens we can proceed with joy, knowing that we are in the will of God.

August 30

God Leads

". . . and the ark of the covenant of the LORD went before them . . ." (Num. 10:33).

The children of Israel were passing through strange territory on their way from Egypt to Canaan, and they had to depend on God to lead them. In the beginning He led them with a pillar of cloud by day and a pillar of fire by night. Later, after the ark of the covenant had been made, the presence of God resided above the mercy seat, and God used the ark to lead His people. When the ark was moved, they moved. When the ark was stopped, they stopped.

We too are passing through strange territory. We have not passed this way before, so we need God to lead us. We are to wait upon God and trust Him to lead us. An old song says it well:

"In shady green pastures, so rich and so sweet,
　God leads His dear children along;
Where the water's cool flow bathes the weary ones' feet,
　God leads His dear children along.
Sometimes on the mount where the sun shines so bright,
　God leads His dear children along;
Sometimes in the valley, the darkest of night,
　God leads His dear children along.
Tho' sorrows befall us, and Satan oppose,
　God leads His dear children along;
Thru grace we can conquer, defeat all our foes,
　God leads His dear children along."

August 31

The Work of the King

"These were the potters, and those that dwelt among plants and hedges: there they dwelt with the king for his work" (1 Chr. 4:23).

Not all of the King's workers are in high places, but that does not mean that their work is not important. The potter trade may not have been an exalted trade, but potters made pots that were useful to ordinary people. They were also useful to kings. Some of their pots were beautiful, and some have survived the ravages of time and are now displayed in great museums.

Like the potters, we may reside among plants and hedges, and our work may seem unimportant. But we are working for the King, and our work is not just for time, it is for eternity.

Our work may last like the shining stars and may one day be on display in the museum of Heaven. So we should never be discouraged, even if we labor at a lowly task among the plants and hedges. Our reward will come after a while.

"And they that be wise shall shine as the brightness of the firmament; and they that turn many to righteousness as the stars for ever and ever" (Dan. 12:3).

Devotions for September

September 1
Children of Light

"Ye are all the children of light, and the children of the day: we are not of the night, nor of darkness" (1 Thess. 5:5).

We have reason to rejoice. We are the children of light. Unsaved people are in Satan's kingdom, and he is the prince of darkness. They love darkness because their deeds are evil. Sadly they will spend eternity in a place of eternal darkness.

God's kingdom is a kingdom of light. He is the source of natural light in the universe, and He is the source of spiritual light. *"God is light, and in him is no darkness at all"* (1 John 1:5).

In Heaven we will not need the light of the sun. God will be the light of that fair land. In Heaven everything is bright and beautiful. The angels shine like the light, and Daniel tells us that soul winners will shine like the stars forever. (Dan. 12:3).

We do not have to wait until we get to Heaven to enjoy the light. As we walk the earthly pathway, God's Word is our light. *"Thy word is a lamp unto my feet, and a light unto my path"* (Psa. 119:105). What a blessed privilege it is to be in the kingdom of light and walk in the light of God's Word.

September 2
Blessed Sleep

"When thou liest down, thou shalt not be afraid: yea, thou shalt lie down, and thy sleep shall be sweet" (Prov. 3:24).

Many do not get enough sleep, and they are always tired. They drag through each day with the assistance of several cups of coffee or other stimulants. That can cause premature aging and may even shorten their life. Our bodies require enough sleep to keep them healthy.

On the other hand, there are those who sleep too much. Too much sleep leads to slothfulness. The writer of Proverbs asked, *"How long wilt thou sleep, O sluggard? . . ."* (Prov. 6:9). Then he added, *"So shall thy poverty come as one that travelleth, and thy want as an armed man"* (verse 11).

Saved people should manage their sleep and their waking hours as well. There must be time to work, and time for recreation. There must be time to pray, time to read the Bible, and time to worship. And there must be time to attend church and to work for the Lord. This is quite a schedule, so we must budget our time.

September 3
Learning to Pray

". . . Lord, teach us to pray . . ." (Luke 11:1).

Jesus lived and walked in a spirit of prayer. He prayed alone. He prayed with His disciples. He prayed in desert places, and He prayed in the midst of throngs of people. It is little wonder that one of the disciples requested that He teach them to pray.

The disciple did not ask Jesus to teach them how

to pray.

People are born with the ability to pray. Hard sinners pray when they are in trouble or when they are facing death. Heathen, in deepest jungles, pray, though they know not to whom they are praying. A simple, "Lord help" is a prayer that can be uttered by a helpless child or by a dying octogenarian.

The request of the disciple goes deeper than how to pray. Their's was an appeal to be taught to practice prayer. We all know how to pray, though our prayer may be uttered with stammering words. Our shortcoming is in making time to worship and commune with our heavenly Father. D. L. Moody said, "If a man is too busy to pray, he is too busy."

September 4

Strength for the Journey

"... *the journey is too great for thee* ..." (1 Kings 19:7).

Elijah's trials had been many. He had delivered God's message of judgment to wicked King Ahab. He had survived the great drought. He had challenged 450 prophets of Baal and had prayed fire down from Heaven. When threatened by Jezebel, he had run 130 miles, then had gone a day's journey into the wilderness. There, weary and despondent, he had prayed to die. Elijah thought he was finished, but God knew he was not.

God loved Elijah in victory on Mt. Carmel, and He loved him in defeat under the juniper tree, praying to die. Conditions do not change God's love.

God provided for Elijah during the drought, and He provided for him under the juniper tree. God knew the journey had been too great for Elijah, and He cared about him.

God did not grant Elijah's request to die. He had greater plans for him than for his bones to bleach beneath the juniper tree. So God arranged a meeting with Elijah on Mount Horeb. On the mountain God demonstrated His power, reassured His prophet, and recommissioned him.

As God cared for Elijah, He cares for us today. He knows when the journey is too great for us, and in our time of need, He wants to meet with us, to encourage us, and to give us guidance.

September 5

The Power of United Prayer

". . . if two of you shall agree on earth as touching any thing that they shall ask, it shall be done for them of my Father which is in heaven. For where two or three are gathered together in my name, there am I in the midst of them" (Matt. 18:19, 20).

There is power in united prayer. Jesus has promised to be in the midst of two or three who are gathered in His name. This does not mean that He will not hear us when we pray alone. He often prayed alone Himself when He was on earth. It does mean that there is an added blessing when we pray with others. Marvelous things often happen when godly people pray together.

Dr. J. Wilbur Chapman became pastor of a great church in Philadelphia in his youth. Mr. Wannamaker, a merchant prince and postmaster general, was a member of the church. After Dr. Chapman became his pastor, Mr. Wannamaker told him that he did not vote for him, because he was afraid he was too young and inexperienced to be pastor of their great church.

However, he promised that he would support him and that he and two other men were going to pray for the power of the Holy Spirit to be upon him. Other men soon joined Mr. Wannamaker and his friends, and in time there were over 200 men praying with him before every service. God answered their prayers, and in three years there were 1100 conversions, including 600 men.

Churches and pastors often fail because the people do not pray. We should pray for our churches and pastors often. We should pray alone, and we should pray with others.

September 6
Clouds That Bless

"If the clouds be full of rain, they empty themselves upon the earth . . ." (Ecc. 11:3).

Clouds may bring bane or blessing. Clouds may cover the sun, but they do not quench its light. Like a fiery chariot, the sun continues to ride across the heavens, and when the clouds are gone its light again shines upon the earth.

The purpose of clouds is to give rain. They draw water from the oceans, lakes, and water courses, lift it on high, and ride upon the winds to dry and thirsty regions and empty themselves. Clouds often look threatening, but they bring blessings upon the earth.

When our clouds are dark and threatening, we should trust in the goodness of God. A dear elderly lady once said in my presence, "We know that God is too wise to make mistakes and too good to be unkind." Instead of expecting the worst, we should look for blessings beyond our trials. Without the clouds we would never see the rainbow of promise. We will never see the valley that lies beyond the mountain until we have climbed the mountain. We cannot see the sunrise until we have passed through the night. Without the clouds there would be no rain.

September 7
Why We Were Born

"*. . . For what is your life? . . .*" (James 4:14).

James places this question between two tremendous truths. 1. We do not know what tomorrow will bring. 2. Life is short, and time is fleeting. These truths rise like mountain peaks. One is the mountain of uncertainty, and the other is the mountain of eternity. These mountains are ever before us. Yesterday is gone, and tomorrow is uncertain. We can only be sure of today, and we should use it wisely.

We have an allotted time—three score and ten years—perhaps a few more years. What shall we do with those years? We should spend them serving God and our fellowman.

Life is a balancing act. How much time do we give to God, and how much time do we spend in our own pursuits? We should have God in our thoughts at the beginning of each day, and we should share flowers of kindness and deeds of service with others as we journey through the day.

> Just one life.
> It will soon be passed.
> Only what we do for Christ will last.
> —Author unknown

September 8
There Is No Substitute for Jesus

"*. . . Lord, to whom shall we go? thou hast the words of eternal life*" (John 6:68).

Eternal life! What staggering words. Man was not created for time alone. He was created for eternity. When a baby is born, it is not cast upon the sea of life in a tiny craft, to drift aimlessly without chart or compass, to be buffeted by winds and waves until at last it crashes upon the rocks of some unknown shore and sinks out of sight as if it had never been. Life is more than that. The poet, Longfellow, put it well when he wrote:

> "Life is real; life is earnest,
>   And the grave is not its goal.
> Dust thou art, to dust returnest
>   Was not spoken of the soul."

Surely we should live for eternity. We should receive Jesus as our Saviour, and we should win every soul to Him that we possibly can.

September 9
The Greatest Gain

"Yea doubtless, and I count all things but loss for the excellency of the knowledge of Christ Jesus my Lord: for whom I have suffered the loss of all things" (Phil. 3:8).

Paul considered what he had lost and what he had gained by becoming a Christian. He had lost position, reputation, friends, possessions, comforts of home, and safety. But he had gained new life in Christ. He was now a citizen of Heaven, and one day he would wear a crown in the presence of his Lord. He reached a conclusion and exclaimed, *"I count all things but loss."* To him the things that we count dear were as nothing, for he had gained eternal life.

Today we do not have to suffer loss as Paul did, but we do have to give up some things. We give up the old life-style, the old habits, and the old sins. We may lose some friends if we are unable to win them to Christ, but, we gain a new nature. We gain a new family. We gain a new purpose in life, and we gain a home in Heaven. Best of all we gain a relationship with Jesus.

Jesus becomes our Saviour, our high priest, our keeper, our guide, and our friend. He is our strength when we are weak, our comforter when we are in sorrow, and our helper when we are in trouble. We can walk with Him through life, knowing that when we walk the last mile, He will walk with us through death, and "We Won't Have to Cross Jordan Alone."

September 10

The Promises of God

*"Whereby are given unto us exce*eding great and precious promises . . ."* (2 Pet. 1:4).

The Bible is filled with promises. In 1 Timothy 4:8 Paul tells us that we have promises for the life that now is and for the life that is to come. There are promises that pertain to the Christian life and promises that pertain to earthly needs. Those promises have been a comfort to the children of God in past ages, and they are no less a comfort to the children of God in the present. Many troubled children of God have pillowed their heads upon those promises in the past, and we can do the same today. As a shipbuilder fashions a ship to conquer the storms at sea, God has given us promises that will enable us to survive the storms of life.

We should search for God's promises in His Word as a miner digs for golden nuggets in the earth. We should read His promises often. We should memorize them. We should believe them. We should rest upon them, and we should share them with others.

September 11
Following God's Leading

"Cause me to hear thy lovingkindness in the morning; for in thee do I trust: cause me to know the way wherein I should walk; for I lift up my soul unto thee" (Psa. 143:8).

We should meet God in the morning. We need to bathe in His loving-kindness, and we need Him to lead us along the untried pathway of the unfolding day.

Each new day is an investment God makes in our lives. We have not passed this way before, and we will never pass this way again. Today's temptations we must reject. Today's opportunities we should claim. Today's blessings we should share.

Looking back over our past lives we see some days that are tarnished. There are days that are pale, and there are days that are black. There are also some bright days. The pale days are days when we accomplished little. The tarnished days were days when we did not do our best. The black days are days when we did something we can never be proud of. The bright days are the days when we did our best for God and for others. As God leads, we should do our best to make this day and all our future days bright and shining.

September 12
The Way of Victory

"For whatsoever is born of God overcometh the world: and this is the victory that overcometh the world, even our faith" (1 John 5:4).

The Gospel of John was written to tell us how to be saved (John 20:31). The first epistle of John was written that we may know that we are saved (1 John 5:13).

We can know that we are saved because Jesus paid for our sins on Calvary. The Bible plainly teaches that when we receive Jesus as our Saviour, He saves us. We should never let the devil win a victory by making us doubt our salvation. We can know that we are saved and know that we know that we are saved. We should never doubt. Doubt brings discouragement. Faith will enable us to live on the victory side every day.

We were not saved to live in doubt and be defeated. We were saved to have victory over the world, the flesh, and the devil. The faith that saved us can give us victory.

We all have our trials, but by faith we can walk over them as Peter walked on the tossing waves of the Sea of Galilee. Peter only got in trouble when he took his eyes off of Jesus and started looking at the wind and the waves. He got out of trouble when he called on Jesus. Like him, we get in trouble when we look at our problems instead of looking unto Jesus, our Saviour and our problem solver.

September 13

Some Day We'll Understand

". . . What I do thou knowest not now; but thou shalt know hereafter" (John 13:7).

Jesus washed the disciples feet to teach them a lesson in humility. Peter, not understanding, objected. Jesus told him that the time would come when he would understand.

Many things come our way that we do not understand. When that happens, we have to walk by faith. Often, with the passing of time, things work out and we come to understand that God has worked it all out for our good and for His glory. Then we can be glad, even thankful, that the trial came our way.

There are things that we will never understand in this life, but we will understand them in the life to come. The following words, written by a songwriter long ago are to the point.

When the Morning Comes

We are often tossed and driven on the restless
    sea of time.
Somber skies and howling tempest oft' succeed
    a bright sunshine.
In that land of perfect day, when the mists have
    rolled away,
We'll understand it better by and by.

September 14

Others

"For whosoever shall give you a cup of water to drink in my name, because ye belong to Christ, verily I say unto you, he shall not lose his reward" (Mark 9:41).

Others may have trials that are greater than ours. Often they bottle their pain inside their hearts, yet we know that they are hurting.

We pass this way but once, so we should do all we can for others along the way. A simple gift, a compliment, or a kind word may accomplish more than we think possible.

Being a Blessing
As we travel on life's way
Let us always do and say
The kind of things that bless
And encourage those in distress.
Flowers we plant along life's road.
May lighten some traveler's load.
Kind things we do and say
Can brighten the darkest day.
                              —Louis Arnold

September 15
Praying in Faith

"*. . . concerning the work of my hands command ye me*" (Isa. 45:11).

The great Jewish evangelist, Dr. Hyman Appelman, was an outstanding preacher and a giant in prayer. He called our text for today to my attention, and it has been a blessing to me.

Many have the habit of ending every prayer with the phrase, "If it be Thy will." That expresses submission, but it can be used as a cover for a lack of faith. If our prayer is not answered, we can always say, "It wasn't the Lord's will."

It is well to end a prayer with, "If it be Thy will," when we are not sure we are praying in the will of God. But we should not use the phrase when we know we are praying in God's will. For example, when we pray for God to save the lost, we know that it is His will, and we should pray in confidence. There are many things we pray for that we know are in the will of God. Let us pray for them in confidence. Certainly this is true concerning the work of God's hands.

September 16
Stand Still When Things Go Wrong

". . . Fear ye not, stand still, and see the salva-tion of the LORD . . ." (Ex. 14:13).

Moses had tremendous problems. Counting women and children, he had taken an estimated 2 million of Pharaoh's slaves out of Egypt. Now Pharaoh was pursuing them with 600 war chariots, and there appeared no way for them to escape. They were hemmed in by the sea and the wilderness. They could not go forward, and they could not go to the left or the right.

The frightened people blamed Moses and started shouting, *". . . it had been better for us to serve the Egyptians, than that we should die in the wilderness"* (Ex. 14:12).

In the midst of the turmoil, Moses shouted, *"Stand still."* Why did he do that? How could he expect the frightened people to stand still with the sound of Pharaoh's chariot wheels were rumbling like thunder in their ears?

The answer is FAITH. Moses was a man of faith. His faith is mentioned five times in Hebrews 11, the great faith chapter of the Bible. No other Bible character is mentioned so often in that chapter.

We may not have faith such as Moses had. Neither do we have trials such as he had. God gave Moses faith for his big trials, and He will give us faith for our trials, whatever their size. We too can stand still and see the salvation of the Lord.

September 17
Go Forward

"And the LORD said unto Moses, Wherefore

criest thou unto me? speak unto the children of Is-rael, that they go forward" (Ex. 14:15).

Moses was told to command the Children of Israel to go forward to escape the approaching Egyptian chariots. Go forward? How could they go forward? The Red Sea was washing at their feet, and it was eighteen miles across.

Moses was told to stretch out his shepherd's staff over the sea, and they were to march toward the sea by faith. It was up to God to make a way for them to cross.

God did make a way for them. The pillar of cloud, that was their guide, moved between them and the Egyptians. It was a cloud of darkness to the Egyptians, but it was a cloud of light to the Isralites.

The sea parted before them, and they walked across on dry ground. When they reached the other side the parted sea came together, and the Egyptians enemies were drowned. Then the Isralites started singing a song of victory.

Our trials are of a different kind, but they are nonetheless real. We just have to learn to walk in God's will and to leave the outcome to Him.

September 18

Thank God for the Thorns

". . . I take pleasure in infirmities, in reproaches, in necessities, in persecutions, in distresses for Christ's sake: for when I am weak, then am I strong" (2 Cor. 12:10).

Paul had learned to take pleasure in things that went wrong. It is easy to be thankful for the bright days, but it is not easy to be thankful for the dark days. We are thankful for the roses but not for the thorns. It is easy to praise God for the sunlit mountain tops, but it is not easy to praise Him for the dark valleys.

Paul had learned from his trials. Often he was beaten until he was weak. In those times he had to depend entirely upon the Lord. Those were the times when he was strong, for the Lord upheld him by His power.

Often bedridden Christians have shining faces and glowing testimonies. Some of them count it a privilege to witness to everyone who enters their sick room. Into such sick rooms I have gone to comfort a suffering one and have come away comforted. I entered to inspire but found that I was the one who needed inspiring. They had learned to make the most of their afflictions. May God help us also to rejoice when we are pricked by the thorns of affliction. With trust in the Lord we can turn our dark days into bright days.

September 19
Songs in the Night

". . . Where is God my maker, who giveth songs in the night" (Job. 35:10).

Job's trials were so great he felt that God was beyond his reach, yet he knew that God can give songs in the night. Job may not have seen the light at the end of the tunnel, but in time God blessed him beyond anything he had known before.

When Shadows Fall

Oft shadows fall,
And then the dark.
The night birds call,
And wild dogs bark.

In sudden fear
A little boy
Held back a tear,
Forgot his toy.

She held him fast
In arms so strong.
As his fear passed,
She sang a song:

When shadows fall
Through passing years.
God hears our call
And dries our tears.
                    —Louis Arnold

God gives songs in the night to comfort us. When our nights are dark and long we can look to Him for comfort.

September 20

Looking on the Bright Side

". . . O LORD; in the morning will I direct my prayer unto thee, and will look up" (Psa. 5:3).

It is good to pray in the morning. Starting our day with prayer will help us through the day. Committing our lives to God will brighten our outlook and that will help us face whatever trials the day may bring.

Dr. Leland Wang, a well-known Chinese evangelist, gave the following testimony after being beaten and robbed by ten bandits:

"My Bible was lost, but not the Christ. My sermon notes were lost, but not the message. My passport was lost, but not the way to Heaven. My address book was lost, but not my friends."

That is an example of counting blessings instead

of worrying over losses. An old songwriter gave good advice when he wrote, *Count Your Blessings.* Countless thousands have been blessed by singing,

> Count your blessings.
> Name them one by one,
> And it will surprise you,
> What the Lord has done.

September 21
Caring about Others

"Look not every man on his own things, but every man also on the things of others" (Phil. 2:4).

This verse means to look after the interest of others just as we look out for our own interest.

In parts of Italy, after a peasant girl is married she starts gathering rose leaves and putting them in a muslin bag she has made. She continues to gather rose leaves year after year, and when she dies the pillow of fragrant rose leaves she has gathered is placed under her head.

It is possible for us, year after year, to gather the rose leaves of tender ministries, unselfish sacrifices, brave actions, and loving deeds. If we let opportunities slip past us, we will not complete our collection of tender memories for our head to rest upon in the final hour. Let us be careful to crowd into our lives lovely, unselfish and helpful things.

—Abbreviated, author unknown

September 22
How to Handle Depression

"Why art thou cast down, O my soul? and why art thou disquieted in me? hope thou in God: for I shall yet praise him . . ." (Psa. 42:5).

The Psalmist was depressed when he wrote the words of our text, but he was not without hope. His hope was in God. He knew that God could handle any problem of the present, and that in time God would give him cause to rejoice.

The Bible tells us that, "*. . . greater is he that is in you, than he that is in the world*" (1 John 4:4). Satan can cause us to be depressed, but God can lift our spirits.

That should give us cause to look beyond the darkness of the present hour, knowing that God will give us brighter days in the future.

Our God is a present help in the time of trouble. He can lift our spirits when we are downcast, and give us cause to hope for brighter days. Like the Psalmist, we can hope in God and look forward to brighter days that will give us cause to praise God.

September 23

What to Do With Our Cares

"Casting all your care upon him; for he careth for you" (1 Pet. 5:7).

We often pick up cares along the way and carry with us. Some of these cares do not even concern us, so we should pass them by. Other cares are responsibilities that we cannot easily lay aside. We can recognize these as privileges, and they will cease to be cares.

It is a privilege to serve others. Think how much you would miss them if they were no longer present so you could do things for them.

Some cares are not really important. We can lay them aside as easily as we picked them up. On the other hand, there are cares that we cannot avoid. These we should cast upon the Lord, knowing that He cares for us. There is nothing too hard for our all-powerful God. After we have taken our cares to Him, we do not need to continue to carry them. We should remember our Lord's promise, *"For my yoke is easy, and my burden is light"* (Matt. 11:30).

September 24

Praise the Lord

"Oh that men would praise the LORD for his goodness, and for his wonderful works to the children of men!" (Psa. 107:8).

It is not difficult to praise God when all is going well, but it takes spiritual maturity to praise Him when things go wrong. In times of trouble it is difficult to remember the blessings of God. One bad day can erase the memory of a thousand good days. When bad days come it is well to remember that God still lives and that He is in control.

Our text gives two reasons for praising God. We are to praise Him for His goodness, and we are to praise Him for the wonderful things He has done. For example, He did wonderful things to make life on earth possible. The earth had to be the right size and the right distance from the sun and the moon. The sun and the moon had to be the right size, and the earth had to be tilted the proper degrees on its axis to make the seasons possible. Without the seasons life on earth would not be possible.

For life to be possible on earth, the earth had to have fertile soil, the right amount of water, and an atmosphere composed of the proper gases in the correct proportions. God created vegetation to breath in carbon dioxide and breath out oxygen. Men and animals breath oxygen and exhale carbon dioxide. That keeps the atmosphere in balance. All of that could not have been an accident. God made it so.

The earth had to contain minerals, metals, fuels, chemicals, and precious stones for man to use, and they had to be in sufficient quantities to last for millenniums. God made plants and trees that would make medicines centuries before man learned to make medicines of his own. Truly we have reason to praise God.

September 25

Pray Always

"Praying always with all prayer and supplication in the Spirit, and watching thereunto with all perseverance and supplication for all saints" (Eph. 6:18).

We live in a world where prayer is always needed. Satan works to detain us, defeat us, derail us, and destroy us. Peter tells us that *". . . the devil, as a roaring lion, walketh about, seeking whom he may devour"* (1 Pet. 5:8).

We should recognize Satan as an enemy, but we should not fear him. We are told to pray that we enter not into temptation (Luke 22:40). We should pray that prayer, knowing that God is greater than the devil. And we should take comfort that the Lord is with us, and that the Holy Spirit is in us. We can pray in the Spirit, as our text tells us, and we should pray for others at all times.

In addition to our regular prayer time, we should

be in an attitude of prayer at all times. We have an open line to Heaven, and we should use it. Our Father is ready to answer when we call.

September 26
Rest in the Lord

"Rest in the LORD, and wait patiently for him: fret not thyself because of him who prospereth in his way . . ." (Psa. 37:7).

It is not possible to be at rest while we are worrying. Worry cancels faith, and destroys peace of mind. Yet there are Christians who worry, fret, and stew much of the time. They have never learned to cast their care upon the Lord and rest in Him.

In the chapter from which our text is taken we are told not to fret because there are wicked people in the world (verse 1). We are told not to fret because sinful people prosper. In due time God's people will be rewarded.

It is not possible to be happy while worrying, nor is it possible for those around us to be happy while we are worrying. Further, it is not possible to serve the Lord as we should if we spend our time fretting and worrying. *"Commit thy works unto the LORD, and thy thoughts shall be established"* (Prov. 16:3).

September 27
Rejoice When Things Go Wrong

"Yet I will rejoice in the LORD, I will joy in the God of my salvation. The LORD God is my strength . . ." (Hab. 3:18, 19).

In the preceding verse the prophet writes of things going wrong. He wrote of the fig tree not blooming, the grapevines not bearing, the olive trees failing, crops in the fields not producing, and the livestock dying. Yet he said he would rejoice because God was his strength.

We should not depend on the things we can see. To often they fail us. Even when it seems that God has forgotten us and there is no deliverance in sight, we should trust in Him and rejoice.

It does not take faith to sail on a calm sea. We do not need faith when all is going well. It is the troubled sea, the dark night, and the deep valleys that requires faith.

When we face trials it is well to remember that others have faced similar trials and have walked through them by faith. God was with them and brought them through their trials when there was no earthly help in view.

It is not easy to rejoice when things go wrong, but we should rejoice anyway. When trials are more than we can handle, we should remember that the Lord is our strength. Nothing is too hard for Him to handle. Knowing that, we can rejoice by faith even when things go wrong.

September 28
Being Doers of the Word

"But be ye doers of the word, and not hearers only, deceiving your own selves" (James 1:22).

The Word of God is comforting, inspiring, and instructive. It is a blessing to read the Word, and it is a joy to hear the Word rightly proclaimed. Yet one can both read and hear the Word and not follow its precepts. We are to be doers of the Word, not hearers only.

It is possible to read the Bible for argument's sake only. Or one can search the Bible for proof texts to support a preconceived idea. In either case this is a misuse of the Bible. The Bible was given for our comfort, guidance, and instruction in righteousness. The Bible is like a letter from home. It contains instructions from our loving heavenly Father. We should read it and live by its instructions.

September 29

God's Books

"The LORD shall count, when he writeth up the people, that this man was born there. Selah" (Psa. 87:6).

God has some books. One of God's books is the Bible. Another is the Book of Life. The names of all the saved are inscribed in it. Many people will never be listed in *Who's Who* in this life, but all who receive Christ as Saviour will be listed in God's Book of Life.

We are told in Revelation 20 that books will be opened at the Great White Throne Judgment. Doubtless, one of these books will be the Book of Record. In that book will be recorded all the details of our life, even the place of our birth. The Bible tells us that even the hairs of our heads are numbered.

Many things that are recorded in the Book of Records will be most embarrassing to the unsaved when Christ comes again, but Christians need have no fear. For the blood of Jesus has blotted out all of their sins. It is wonderful to know that all our sins are blotted out of God's Book of Records. It is even more wonderful to know that our names will never be blotted out of the Book of Life.

September 30
Better Things to Come

". . . in whom also after that ye believed, ye were sealed with that holy Spirit of promise, Which is the earnest of our inheritance until the redemption of the purchased possession, unto the praise of his glory" (Eph. 1:13, 14).

The word *"earnest,"* used in our text, means the down payment or the guarantee of future payments to be made. The Holy Spirit, who indwells believers and by whom believers are sealed, is the guarantee of better things to come. We have many blessings from the Holy Spirit in this life, and He is the earnest of things to come in the future life.

In this life we have the fruit of the Spirit, *". . . love, joy, peace, longsuffering, gentleness, goodness, faith, Meekness, temperance: against such there is no law"* (Gal. 5:22-23). Better things are yet to come. There is coming the "redemption of the purchased property. *"For ye are bought with a price . . ."* (1 Cor. 6:20).

Our soul has been redeemed, and one day our bodies will be redeemed. After that, there will be no sin, no sickness, and no death. We will have bodies like our Lord's glorious body, and we will enjoy Heaven forever. Better things are yet to come.

Devotions for October

October 1
The Lighted Pathway

"But the path of the just is as the shining light, that shineth more and more unto the perfect day" (Prov. 4:18).

Unsaved people walk in paths of darkness, and darkness follows in their wake. Those who follow them walk in darkness also, and that darkness leads to a place of eternal darkness.

Saved people walk in paths of light, and they leave a trail of light behind them. The pathway they follow grows brighter as they approach the Land of Perfect Day. Even after they have gone to that Land their afterglow remains. Eternity alone will tell of all who have been led to trust Christ as Saviour by the light of a departed loved one.

Saved people can walk in the light, because Jesus came into this dark world to light the way for them. He walked a dark path to the cross. He went into the darkness of the tomb, but He came out at the first light of the third day. He had conquered death, hell, and the grave and had made a lighted pathway for us to follow. We can walk in the light with Him and have continual cleansing (John 1:7). Also, as we walk in the light, we have fellowship with other Christians.

October 2
Letting God Take Charge

"Commit thy way unto the Lord; trust also in him; and he shall bring it to pass" (Psa. 37:5).

When things go wrong for us, instead of trying to work them out on our own, we should commit them to God, knowing that *". . . he shall bring it to pass."*

A young pastor had done everything he knew to do but had failed. So he decided to give up his church and quit the ministry. Then God seemed to say to him, "Son, you have tried and failed. Why don't you trust me to bless your ministry instead of trying to do everything by yourself?" The young preacher decided to continue in the ministry and trust God to do what he could not do. After that he succeeded beyond his fondest dreams. It remains to be seen what God will do with our lives if we will let Him be in charge.

October 3
Active Faith

"And she went up, and laid him on the bed of the man of God, and shut the door upon him, and went out" (2 Kings 4:21).

In an article on this verse, C. H. Mackintosh points out that the Shunammite woman of our verse for to-day is one of the most striking illustrations in the Bible of how we should commit our troubles to God. The son God had given her had died, but she did not spend time mourning. Instead, she took her dead son up to the room she and her husband had built for the prophet, Elisha. Perhaps she thought that the presence of God must abide in the room where the man of God had slept. She left her dead son in the room and went to get Elisha. That was an act of faith.

When Elisha saw her coming, he asked if all was well with her, and her husband and her child. All was not well. Her child was dead, but by faith she answered, "It is well."

The man of God returned home with her and performed one of the great miracles of the Old Testament. God rewarded her faith, and Elisha raised her son from the dead.

The Shunammite woman lived in a different land and in a different time from ours, but she served the same God that we serve. God honored her faith, and He honors faith today. We can close the door upon our troubles and trust in God.

October 4
The Blessed Holy Spirit

"Howbeit when he, the Spirit of truth, is come, he will guide you into all truth: for he shall not speak of himself . . . and he will shew you things to come" (John 16:13).

It is well to remember that the Holy Spirit is not a mere power or influence. The Holy Spirit is the third person of the Godhead.

The following quote from Dr. R. A. Torrey, an associate of D. L. Moody, is to the point. "If you think of the Holy Spirit, as so many Christian people do today, as a mere influence or power, then your thought will constantly be, how can I get hold of the Holy Spirit and use it? But if you think of Him in the Biblical way as a person of divine majesty and glory, your thought will be, How can the Holy Spirit get hold of me and use me? There is a vast difference between the thought of man, the worm, using God to thresh the mountain, and God using man, the worm, to thresh the mountain."

October 5
The Word of God

"But he answered and said, It is written, Man shall not live by bread alone, but by every word that proceedeth out of the mouth of God" (Matt. 4:4).

There is a tradition that the descendants of Seth lived on the summit of such a lofty mountain they could hear the singing of the heavenly hosts and could even join in the singing. That is only an old story, but let us think of the Bible as that high mountain. The Word of God begins on earth and reaches to the throne of God.

The Bible is practical in this world. It gives us the way of salvation; it nourishes our spiritual lives; it builds our faith; it feeds our spiritual nature; it is a bridge over troubled waters, and it teaches us right from wrong. The Bible does even more than that. It gives us visions of the Land that is fairer than day, and it tells us to lay up treasures in that Land. It also tells us to do works that will earn rewards and give us crowns of recognition in the glory world.

October 6
Life Is Worth Living

"And the LORD God formed man of the dust of the ground, and breathed into his nostrils the breath of life; and man became a living soul" (Gen. 2:7).

Life is a gift from God. It is the only life we will ever have. We should treasure it, live it joyfully, and honor God with every day that He gives us.

We should never give up on life. William Cowper, a great hymn writer, walked the banks of the Seine River in Paris four times intending to end his life, but he did not plunge in. Three times he filled a cup with poison, but he did not drink it. Twice he cocked a pistol and placed it against his temple, but he did not pull the trigger. Despite mental anguish, William Cowper found life worth living. He lived to become a highly regarded poet. Millions have been blessed by his writings. A verse of one of his poems follows.

> God moves in mysterious ways,
>   His wonders to perform;
> He plants His footsteps in the sea,
>   And rides upon the storm.

Life is worth living. Thank God for it and treasure it. Only time will tell what you will be able to accomplish if you invest your time and your talent wisely.

October 7
Only Believe

"And Jesus answering saith unto them, Have faith in God" (Mark 11:22).

One day Jesus went to a fig tree to get some figs and found it barren. He promptly pronounced judgment on the barren tree. The next day when He and His disciples were passing that way, they noticed that the leaves on the tree were dried. Peter remarked about it, and the Lord said to him, *" . . . Have faith in God."*

There are two lessons here. If Jesus would not tolerate a barren fig tree, surely He must be displeased when our lives are barren. The second lesson is that faith brings results.

A man once asked the great prayer-warrior, George Mueller, how to have strong faith. George Mueller replied, "The only way to learn strong faith is to endure great trials. I have learned my faith by standing firm amid severe testings."

When we have trials we should learn from them.

Our trials can build our faith and give us strength to endure future trials. Peter wrote, *"That the trial of your faith, being much more precious than of gold that perisheth, though it be tried with fire, might be found unto praise and honour and glory at the appearing of Jesus Christ"* (1 Pet. 1:7).

October 8
The Value of Prayer with Tears

". . . Thus saith the LORD . . . I have heard thy prayer, I have seen thy tears . . ." (Isa. 38:5).

God heard the prayer, and He saw the tears of sick King Hezekiah. Then God healed him and granted him another fifteen years of life.

When we have cause to weep, our tears count as much as the words of our prayer. Prayer is the golden stairway we can climb to lay our petitions at Heaven's gate. Our tears are the measure of our intensity. God weighs our prayers and counts our tears. Neither our prayers or our tears go unnoticed.

In answer to a letter requesting a copy of a public prayer Henry Ward Beecher had made, he wrote:

"If you will send me the notes of the oriole that it whistled from the tops of my trees last June, or a segment of the rainbow last week, or the perfume of the first violet that blossomed last May, I will send you the prayer that rose to my lips on that occasion and left me forever. I hope it went Heavenward and was registered, in which case the only record of it will be in Heaven."

October 9
Cause to Rejoice

"Let all those that seek thee rejoice and be glad in thee . . ." (Psa. 70:4).

One of the meanings of the word glad is to be bright and cheerful. To rejoice means that one is full of joy. God's people should be full of joy, and they should have a bright and cheerful countenance.

We have reasons to rejoice and be glad because our sins are gone. We have all sinned, but Jesus has cleansed us of all our sins, and we can rejoice that our names are written in the Lamb's Book of Life. We can also rejoice because we have a home in Heaven.

We should rejoice because we have the privilege of serving God. There was a time when we served the devil, and he was a hard taskmaster. He paid us with disappointment, pain, suffering, and the promise of eternal death. Now that we are serving God, we enjoy His blessings, and we have the promise of eternal life in a wonderful place called Heaven. For all of this we should rejoice and be glad.

October 10
Meeting God in the Morning

"And be ready in the morning, and come up . . . present thyself there to me in the top of the mount" (Ex. 34:2).

> Thank God for each new day,
> And seek His guidance in the way.
> Your day will be brighter,
> And your heart will be lighter
> When you take time to pray.
> —Louis Arnold

God asked Moses to meet Him on the mountain. We too should meet God on our mountaintops if we expect Him to meet us in our valleys.

We should meet God in prayer and worship each morning. In today's busy world that is not always easy.

Demands upon our time keep us rushing here and there, and before we realize it our time for meeting God has slipped away. When that happens we need to take the first opportunity to have our quiet time alone with Him.

Driving alone in rush hour traffic, our car can become our secret closet of prayer. We can turn off the radio, and, with eyes wide open to watch for traffic, we can pray to God. We can also make up for lost time by praying silently in quiet moments through the day. Also, we can meet God when we kneel by our bedside at the end of the day.

October 11

We Shall Live Again

"If a man die, shall he live again? . . ." (Job 14:14).

"For I know that my redeemer liveth . . . yet in my flesh shall I see God" (Job 19:25, 26).

Job raises a most important question. If the answer to his question is negative, the sun of hope has gone down and will never rise again. The rainbow of promise has faded from the sky, and the storm-cloud has no silver lining. The last ray of hope has faded from the horizon of the future, and we are of all creatures most miserable.

In great trial and anxiety of soul, Job asked the question, *"If a man die, shall he live again? . . ."* Then in triumphant faith he answered, *". . . in my flesh shall I see God."* He knew that his Redeemer lived, that death was a defeated foe, and that he would live again.

We have more light today than Job had in his day. He did not have a Bible, but we have the Bible with all the promises of God in its pages. We know that our Redeemer lives and that one day we shall see Him face to face. That gives meaning and purpose to life, and it makes life worth living. Isaac Watts expressed it well:

> Jesus shall reign where'er the sun
> Doth his successive journeys run;
> His kingdom spread from shore to shore,
> Till moons shall wax and wane no more.
> —Isaac Watts

October 12
Guardian Angels Are Real

"The angel of the Lord encampeth round about them that fear him, and delivereth them" (Psa. 34:7).

Angels are created beings. We are not told when they were created, but apparently they were created in the morning of creation. Job tells us that the angels shouted for joy when the morning stars sang together (Job 38:7). Angels are powerful, shining beings, and there are too many of them to count. How comforting it is to know that they encamp around us. The Bible speaks of the guardian angels of children (Matt. 18:10).

Angels travel from earth to Heaven and from Heaven to earth, as Jacob saw them ascending and descending upon a ladder. Enough angels remain on earth at all times to encamp around all the children of God. Apparently they watch over us and help us in ways we do not understand. Their guardianship is an evidence of our Father's love and concern for His children.

We live in a wicked world that is controlled by a wicked devil. So we need these angels to watch over us. But we are not to worship angels or even to become acquainted with them. Instead we are to praise God.

Angels know things about us that we do not know, and they are able to do things for us that we cannot do for ourselves.

October 13
Blessed of God

"O taste and see that the LORD is good: blessed is the man that trusteth in him" (Psa. 34:8).

The word blessed is used at least 47 times in the book of Psalms, and it is used 53 times in the four Gospels. One of the definitions of blessed is, bringing happiness, pleasure, or contentment. When the word is used in the Bible, I believe it means blessed by God.

The first three verses of the first Psalm is a good example. There we are told that the man who lives right and delights in and meditates upon the law of the Lord will be like a fruitful tree with evergreen leaves, and that he will prosper in all that he does. That kind of person is blessed indeed.

It is wonderful to feel the good hand of the Lord upon us in blessing as we go about our daily tasks. Surely we should begin each day by praising Him, and we should have praise in our hearts throughout the day. After a day spent serving and praising the Lord, we can say with the Psalmist, *"I will both lay me down in peace, and sleep: for thou, LORD, only makest me dwell in safety"* (Psa. 4:8).

October 14
God Can Calm Our Storms

"He maketh the storm a calm . . ." (Psa. 107:29).

This promise is taken from a passage about storms at sea. The preceding verse says, *"Then they cry unto the LORD in their trouble, and he bringeth them out of their distresses."*

That is what happened to the disciples when they called upon Jesus when they were caught in a storm at sea. Jesus arose, rebuked the wind, and calmed the storm. We should learn from that account to call upon the Lord when we face the storms of life.

Facing Our Storms

Light fades as storm clouds darken.
　　Driven by winds they cross our sky.
Then it is time for us to harken,
　　To comforting Words from on high.
"Fear not when storm clouds thicken,
　　My child, I know and understand.
Be thou not with anguish stricken.
　　I hold your future in my hand."
　　　　　　　　　　—Louis Arnold

October 15
Walking in God's Will

"THERE is therefore now no condemnation to them which are in Christ Jesus, who walk not after the flesh, but after the Spirit" (Rom. 8:1).

We are not saved by walking straight. We are saved so we can walk straight. The carnal nature will not submit to the will of God, but when we are born-again we get a new nature, and the new nature delights to walk in the will of God. We do not walk in the will of God out of a sense of duty. We walk in His will because we love Him.

Years ago, I heard the matchless Gipsy Smith preach. He loved the Lord, and he loved the souls of men. He was 84 years old at the time. He had crossed the ocean 35 times to preach in America. His trip back to England at the end of his eighteenth preaching tour in America would make 36 crossings of the Atlantic.

One night Gipsy Smith said, "I have walked intimately with the Lord for many years. Tonight I sense that He is pleased with the service, and He is going to bless." That may not be a verbatim quote, but it is close to what he said. His statement made me want to walk intimately with the Lord, and to lead others to walk intimately with Him.

Christian have a choice. We can be nominal Christians, go to church, live clean lives, and do the things we are supposed to do without being really close to the Lord. Or we can walk in close fellowship with Him. We should walk the walk every day. That is the path of joy and blessings.

October 16
We Need the Church

"Not forsaking the assembling of ourselves together, as the manner of some is . . ." (Heb. 10:25).

Missing church services can be the first step toward spiritual decline. A turn away from church is a turn toward the world. The world is abrasive to spirituality, and it soon sands away our testimony when we spend time in worldly pursuits. We need to attend spiritual church services to recharge our spiritual batteries. Regular church attendance should be a lifelong habit.

Lack of church attendance will lead to spiritual decline, and that will lead to our becoming backslidden in heart. It is not far from being backslidden in heart to becoming backslidden in behavior.

A pastor became concerned about a member who had stopped attending church and decided to visit him. He found the wayward brother seated before an open fire and received a reluctant invitation to come in and join him. The pastor entered and sat down before the fire. For several minutes he said nothing. The host was uncomfortable, for he knew why the pastor had come to visit him.

At last the pastor took the tongs and lifted a blazing coal from the fire and laid it on the hearth. The coal soon stopped burning, then slowly lost its glow.

"You don't have to say a word, pastor," the wayward brother said. "I'll be in church next Sunday."

October 17

Shared Glory

"And that he might make known the riches of his glory on the vessels of mercy, which he had afore prepared unto glory" (Rom. 9:23).

We are God's vessels of mercy. We were not worthy to be saved, but He saved us by His grace, and He is fitting us for glory. We will have glory in Heaven, but we can also be reflections of God's glory in this world.

A vessel finds its own place. Fitted for cooking, it finds its way to the kitchen. Fitted for beauty, it finds its place in the reception room. Fitted for flowers, it is filled with beauty and fragrance and placed upon a dining table that is set with the finest china and flatware and loaded with the choicest of foods. As vessels of mercy, God can use us to show the riches of His glory.

Glory awaits us in Heaven, but we can experience the glory of God in the present world. God wants us to walk close to Him so He can fill our lives with glory. As vessels of mercy we are permitted to walk in the glory of God every day. Walking with God makes life worth living, and it makes us a testimony to others.

October 18
Rejoice in the Lord

"Rejoice in the Lord alway: and again I say, Rejoice" (Phil. 4:4).

The joy of the Lord is our birthright, and we should never lose it. If we lose our joy we become defeated, and we become a poor advertisement for the Lord. No one wants a long-faced, dreary, complaining religion. God tells us. *". . . neither be ye sorry; for the joy of the LORD is your strength"* (Neh. 8:10).

When the Israelites began to doubt and complain on their way to the Promised Land, they were turned back and had to spend 40 years wandering in the wilderness. The same is true today. Many of God's people are wandering in the wilderness of doubt and despair.

It is not possible to doubt and rejoice at the same time. Faith in God drives out doubt, just as light drives away darkness. When the darkness is gone light prevails. When doubt is gone, rejoicing will prevail.

October 19
The Sign of the Rainbow

"I do set my bow in the cloud, and it shall be for a token of a covenant between me and the earth" (Gen. 9:13).

The rainbow is known by many names. The Italians call it, *The Flashing Arch.* In Sanskrit it is, *The Bow of Indra.* The people of Annam call it, *The Little Window in the Sky.* Some North American tribes greet the rainbow as, *The Bride of the Rain.* In various countries of Central Europe the rainbow is called, *The Arch of Saint Martin, The Bride of the Holy Spirit, The Crown of Saint Barnard, and The Girdle of God.* Many in America speak of a pot of gold at the foot of the rainbow. The rainbow is none of these. It is the sign of God's promise. God promised to look upon the rainbow and remember His covenant with man (Gen. 9:16).

When we see a rainbow it is well to remember that God is also seeing it and remembering His promise to never again destroy the earth with a flood.

The rainbow embodies all the colors of the spectrum. All the colors, when reflected, are pure white light. That reminds us that Jesus is the Light of the world.

We should never see a rainbow without remembering that God placed it in the heavens to tell us of judgment passed and to promise that He will never again destroy the earth with water. Just so, when we receive Jesus as our Saviour our judgment is past, and we will never have to face future condemnation.

October 20
We Shall Be Transformed

". . . we know that, when he shall appear, we shall be like him; for we shall see him as he is" (1 John 3:2).

When John Ruskin was asked, "What is Mud?" he replied: "First of all mud is clay and sand, and usually soot and a little water. When God takes it in hand, He transforms the clay into a sapphire, for a sapphire is just that; and the sand into an opal, for that is the analysis of an opal; and the soot into a diamond, for a diamond is just carbon which has been transformed, and the soiled water into bright snow crystals, for that is what they are when God takes the water up in the clouds and sends it back again."

Man was created from the dust of the ground. When he fell even lower than the dust from which he was made, God intervened and sent His Son to redeem all who would believe on Him. A redeemed person is given a new nature and the opportunity to develop and grow and be transformed to the Lord's own image.

When life's race is over and we move across the river to meet our dear Saviour on the other side, we shall be like Him for we shall see Him as He is. Then, at last, we shall be truly transformed.

October 21
Our Riches in Christ

"*. . . he was rich, yet for your sakes he became poor, that ye through his poverty might be rich*" (2 Cor. 8:9).

The first part of our text speaks of the riches of Christ before He came to earth. He was rich in health, rich in eternal life, and rich in the power of creation. If He had wanted another galaxy He could have created it. He was rich in His relationship with the Father, rich in the company of angels, and rich in the company of redeemed saints.

The second part of our text speaks of Christ's condescendence. He laid aside His royal robe and crown, left by Heaven's gate and entered this world through a barn door. His mother wrapped Him in swaddling clothes, and laid Him in a manger. He had been rich, but he became poor.

The third part of the text speaks of the riches He came to give us. He came so poor lost sinners could be saved and made rich. He loved us when we were unworthy. He called us when we were unwilling, and saved us when we were unable to save ourselves.

Our riches includes eternal life, fellowship with other Christians, the privilege of prayer and worship, and a home in Heaven. Thank God for our riches in Christ Jesus.

October 22
Peace Unbounded

"And the peace of God, which passeth all understanding, shall keep your hearts and minds through Christ Jesus" (Phil. 4:7).

We can experience the peace of God that is beyond understanding. In the midst of turmoil, when we have every reason to be upset, God's peace can fills our hearts. While others are falling under smaller trials they may wonder at our serenity, not knowing that the peace of God sustains us.

There is much that we cannot understand. We cannot fully understand God's power, His Glory, His love, or the things that He has prepared for those that love Him. Paul expressed it well when he wrote, *". . . now I know in part; but then shall I know even as also I am known"* (1 Cor. 13:12).

There's More

We only see a little of the ocean,
    A few miles distance from the rocky shore;
But oh, out there beyond—beyond the horizon
    There's more—there's more!

We only see a little of God's loving,
    A few rich treasures from His mighty store;
But oh, out there beyond life's horizon
    There's more—there's more!
                    —Author Unknown

October 23

The Dwelling Place

"Yea, the sparrow hath found an house, and the swallow a nest . . ." (Psa. 84:3).

The Psalmist wrote about sparrows and swallows to show that God has made it so they can find places to live and rear their young. He went on to write about our dwelling place in the Lord. In verse 4 he wrote, *"Blessed are they that dwell in thy house: they will be still praising thee. Selah."*

Dwelling in the house of the Lord means that we can live in His presence. He is our loving heavenly Father, and He wants us to love Him in return. When trouble comes our way He is our shelter in the time of storm and our rock in a weary land.

Jesus spoke of sparrows to show that God cares for them even though they are of little value. In Luke 12:6 He said, *"Are not five sparrows sold for two farthings* (six-eights of a cent), *and not one of them is forgotten before God?"* In Matthew 10:31 He said, *"Fear ye not therefore, ye are of more value than many sparrows."*

God's loving care gives us reason to praise Him.

October 24

Our Refuge

"For thou hast been . . . a refuge from the storm . . ." (Isa. 25:4).

Spurgeon once saw a weather vane on a barn with the text, *"God is Love"* beneath it. He told the farmer who owned the barn that it was not appropriate, because the love of God never changes. The farmer replied, "You don't get it. What I mean is that no matter which way the wind blows, God still loves us."

The Bible tells us *". . . God is love; and he that dwelleth in love dwelleth in God . . . "* (1 John 4:16).

God's love does not change with the weather, nor does it change because of conditions in the world. We can depend on God's love, and by faith we can ride out the storms of life. No matter what conditions may be, God loves us. We can trust in Him in the calm and in the storm.

October 25

The Value of a Day

"Every day will I bless thee; and I will praise thy name for ever and ever" (Psa. 145:2).

"Yesterday, today was tomorrow. Two days ago yesterday was yet to come. Beyond the horizon it stood, for many never to dawn, for us who are here, it was to come and to pass, a little incident in our cosmical time to add or to subtract from the fair temple of life we are all building."

—Author unknown

It seems that only yesterday we were children. We often look back and wish that we had lived differently, and that we had done more for our Lord. The past is gone, and we cannot relive it, but we can make the most of today and of our future days. In time our bodies will grow weak, but our spirits can grow stronger. It is possible that we can accomplish more for the Lord in our later years than we did with all the rushing and struggling of our younger years.

October 26

God Is Creator

"IN the beginning God created the heaven and the earth" (Gen. 1:1).

God is the creator of all things, and He is the source of all that is good, and worthwhile, and noble. He is our source in life and our hope for the future.

Years ago the great evangelist, Sam Jones, wrote: "Oh, where in all the universe is God's great storehouse of colors from which the rainbow gets its every hue and each blushing flower its tints? The answer comes back, 'I know not.' Oh, where in the universe is God's great storehouse of music from which every warbling bird gets its melodies? from which all the spheres are supplied with their harmonies? And again the answer comes back, 'I know not.'

"In the better, sweeter moments of life, I have asked, 'Oh, where is the great storehouse of God's love, from which every mother gets her love for her children, and every father his love for his home, and every brother his love for his sister, and every husband his love for his wife. The answer comes back, 'It is the great heart of God pouring itself out like a gushing river into every human heart in the world.'"

October 27

We Should be Sincere

"Woe unto you, scribes and Pharisees, hypocrites! . . . and for a pretence make long prayer . . ." (Matt. 23:14).

Hypocrites are people who pretend to be something that they are not. Some hypocrites pretend to be Christians, because they want the recognition Christians get. That tells us that Christians are worthwhile. No one counterfeits pennies, because they are almost worthless. Twenty dollar bills are often counterfeited because they have value.

Some who have never been saved try to copy the

life-style of true Christians. Instead of trusting Jesus as their Saviour, they put up a front. They try to fool others, but usually they do not succeed. Like the Pharisees of Christ's time, they make the outside of the cup clean while the inside remains dirty. Lost people cannot change their hearts. Only Jesus can do that. The Bible makes it clear that only the blood of Jesus cleanses from sin, and the only way to become a Christian is to receive Him as Saviour.

There are no counterfeit infidels. They are not worth copying. Some infidels like to parade their unbelief, and they pretend that not believing in God makes them happy. They even try to convert others to their way of thinking. Do what they will, they are still not worth counterfeiting.

October 28

We Need Not Fear

"But he saith unto them, It is I; be not afraid" (John 6:20).

On a stormy night the disciples were in a ship bound for Capernaum. There was little light, but, as they battled the storm, they were able to see someone walking on the water. The figure was approaching their ship, and they were afraid. What they were seeing could only be a spirit, they thought. They did not realize that Jesus was coming to them in their time of need.

Jesus knew they were afraid, and to reassure them, He said, *". . . It is I; be not afraid."*

The late evangelist, Dr. Hyman Appelman, often used the following illustration:

A small boy walked through a cemetery to attend an afternoon birthday party. Late in the afternoon he

excused himself, saying that he wanted to go home
so he would not have to go back through the cemetery alone after dark.

The lady of the house persuaded him to stay on
and enjoy the party and her husband would walk him
home when the party was over. When the party ended,
she again told the boy that her husband would walk
him home.

"Never mind, ma'am. My big brother has come
after me, so I'm not afraid to walk home in the dark,"
he told her.

Jesus is our elder brother, and He walks with us,
even in the darkness and in the storm, so we need
never be afraid.

October 29
What God Is Like

*"Who (Jesus) is the image of the invisible God,
the firstborn of every creature"* (Col. 1:15).

God is invisible, but we can see Him with our
spiritual eyes. We are told that Moses *". . . endured,
as seeing him who is invisible"* (Heb. 11:27). The
Bible often speaks of seeing and hearing with our
spiritual eyes and ears. Such seeing and hearing is
possible by faith.

Jesus was visible while He was on earth, and He
said, *". . . he that hath seen me hath seen the Father
. . . "* (John 14:9). To know what God is like, we need
to know what Jesus was like.

God is all-powerful. So is Jesus. God is all-wise.
So is Jesus. God is love. So is Jesus. God is so mighty
we can never fully comprehend His greatness while
we are in this life, but knowing Jesus makes it possible for us to know something of what He is like.

In Genesis 1:26 we have God saying, *". . . Let us make man in our image, after our likeness . . ."* Since man is in the image of God, that means that in some way God is like us. Jesus was in the image of man. Knowing Him will help us understand what God is like.

We have spiritual discernment and intelligence far beyond any creature on earth. In those ways, even fallen man is in the likeness of God. It is folly to believe that we were created in the image of dumb beasts. God is a spirit, and He created man as a living soul. Realizing that we are spiritual beings helps us to understand something of what God is like.

October 30
Where Our Affections Should Be

"Love not the world, neither the things that are in the world . . ." (1 John 2:15).

Strange statement: *"Love not the world."* God made the world beautiful for us, and He intends for us to enjoy it. We can enjoy the birth of a new day and the glory of the sunset. We can enjoy the beauty and fragrance of flowers and the songs of the birds. We can enjoy ornaments of gold and the flashing varicolored lights of beautiful jewels. We can enjoy our homes and the conveniences man has made from materials God placed on the earth. Then why are told not to love the world?

We are not to love the world in the sense of worshiping it. We are to love God who made the world. Every blessing the world affords should fill our hearts with praise and cause us to love and worship God.

This world is not our final home. We are just passing through it on our way to a better country. While in the world, we should walk humbly before our God, and we should lay up treasures in our eternal home. *"For where your treasure is, there will your heart be also"* (Matt. 6:21).

October 31
What Is Your Life?

"For me to live is Christ, and to die is gain" (Phil. 1:21).

It is well for us to pause and ask ourselves, "What is the purpose of my life?" Some would have to answer, "For me to live is money." Other would say, "I live for the things money can buy." In either case the life would be wasted. Money and things do not bring happiness or peace of mind, and when we leave this world we will leave everything we own behind.

There are those who live for popularity or for fame. Some live for entertainment. Some live for the pleasures of sin. On and on the list goes, but whatever the reason for living, life is without meaning if we live only for ourselves.

When we live for Christ, life is an investment. We grow to be Christ like, and we live to be a blessing to others. Our home is in Heaven, and our treasures are there. Paul must have had this in mind when he wrote, *". . . to die is gain."*

Devotions for November

November 1
Persevering in Prayer

"Ask, and it shall be given you; seek, and ye shall find; knock, and it shall be opened unto you" (Matt. 7:7).

It is good to know that God has promised that when we ask we shall receive. Our God is a prayer answering God, but sometimes a prayer is not answered at once. When that happens we need to go a second mile or even a third mile in prayer. We need to go beyond simply asking and seek and knock.

Sometimes circumstances can help us understand why our prayers are delayed. Other times we have no idea why the answer does not come. In those times we need to keep on praying and believing.

God may delay the answer to our prayer because we are not ready to receive what we have prayed for. Or God may be preparing the way for an answer that will come in due time. The answer may also be delayed because Satan is hindering. In Daniel chapter 10, we read that Daniel fasted and prayed for 21 days without his prayer being answered. Then, he was told in a vision that his prayer had been heard the first day, but the answer had been hindered by the prince of Persia. Only after the angel, Michael, came to help was his prayer answered.

We are told to ask, to seek, and to knock. That means that we are to pray earnestly and keep on praying. It also means that we are to draw near to God. We are promised that if we draw near to God, He will draw near to us (James 4:8). We need to be close enough to Him to knock on the gate of Heaven.

November 2
Unbelief Is Folly

"THE fool hath said in his heart, There is no God . . ." (Psa. 14:1).

An evolutionist has to believe a lot of unreasonable things. He has to believe in creation without a creator, intelligent design without a designer, energy without a source, and life without one to give life. He has to believe that man has an innate desire to worship without a reason, and he cannot explain why faith in God changes people's lives and gives them peace and happiness. Nor can he explain why faith in God causes people to spend their lives serving Him and working to help others.

Dr. B. R. Lakin used to tell of an infidel who asserted, "There is no God," and a small boy called to him and said, "The Bible says, 'The fool has said in his heart that there is no God,' and you've done blabbed it with your big mouth."

Unbelief does not bring peace. Faith in God brings peace and changes lives. Those who have faith are a blessing to others. Unbelief does none of these things.

November 3
What to Do with Life's Burdens

"Cast thy burden upon the LORD, and he shall sustain thee . . ." (Psa. 55:22).

Years ago in China there were shelves along the roads for the relief of Chinese men and women who served as coolies. They often carried such great burdens that someone had to help put them on their backs at the beginning of the day. If they put them down to rest they could not pick them up again. So when they reached one of the shelves beside the road they backed up to it and rested their burden on it. Jesus is our shelf beside life's road. We can cast our burden upon Him, knowing that He cares for us. Casting our burden upon the Lord makes a heavy task lighter.

Years ago I heard a blacksmith who worked in a coal mine give the following testimony. He said, "I used to arrive at the shop on Monday morning, look around at all the work I had to do and start swearing. I was mad at everybody, and I would swear at everyone who came near me. I was miserable, and I made everyone around me miserable. After I got saved, my entire outlook changed. Now I praise God that I have work to do and that I have the health to do it. People used to shun me, but now they like to be around me." It pays to serve Jesus.

November 4

The Protection of Heaven

"He brought me to the banqueting house, and his banner over me was love" (Song of Solomon 2:4).

Shortly before the beginning of the Spanish-American War a man came from England to America, then went to Cuba. After the war broke out he was arrested by the Spanish as a spy and condemned to be shot. The man was innocent, and the consuls of both the United States and England demanded that he be released.

The Spanish replied, "He was tried in our courts and found guilty, so he must die."

They dug the man's grave and placed his coffin beside it. The soldiers were there, awaiting the order to fire upon the man. Just as the Spanish were covering the man's eyes, up the road came the American and the English consuls. They leaped from their carriage, rushed to the man, and wrapped him in the Star-Spangled Banner and the Union Jack. Then turning to the officer in command they said, "Fire upon those flags if you dare." They did not dare, for those two flags represented two powerful governments.

As God's children we have greater protection than any government on earth can provide. We have the protection of the One who said, *" . . . All power is given unto me in heaven and in earth"* (Matt. 28:18). Even when our time comes to die, we have His promise that we shall live again. Every day we can live in God's banquet house with His banner of love over us.

November 5
We Are Never Alone

". . . lo, I am with you alway, even unto the end of the world. Amen" (Matt. 28:20).

The Lord's promise to be with His children is true in all ages. He was with the disciples in the first century. He has been with His children in all the past centuries, and He will be with them until the end of the age. After the end of the age we will be with Him.

Jesus knows our trials. He lived in the flesh and suffered trials as we do. Until He was thirty years old He worked in a carpenter shop in Nazareth. Like other carpenters He was often wet with perspiration and covered with sawdust. He suffered the same discomforts as other carpenters. He understands the trials we suffer as we work today.

The Bible tells us that He was tempted at all points as we are. Because He was tempted, He understands when we are tempted, and He gives us strength for the journey.

In the beginning of our verse for today, Jesus told His disciples that all power was given to Him in Heaven and on earth. Then He told them to go into all the world to make converts, to baptize them, and to teach them. He promised to be with them till the end of the age. That means that He is with us as we serve Him today.

November 6
Importance of the Right Attitude

"For as he (a person) *thinketh in his heart, so is he . . ."* (Prov. 23:7).

In the early eighteen hundreds there lived in England two great writers who were both lame. Their names were Lord Byron and Sir Walter Scott. Scott never complained about his condition, but Byron complained, grumbled, moaned and protested everywhere he went. He was miserable, and he made everyone around him miserable.

Scott was a man of high spirits and good cheer, and he was welcomed everywhere he went. He knew the Lord. Apparently Byron did not. In Byron's latter years he wrote:

> My days are in the yellow leaf,
>   The flowers and fruit of life are gone.
> The worm, the canker, and the grief
>   Are mine alone.

Sir Walter Scott sang everywhere he went. Like John Greenleaf Whittier he could say:

I know not where His islands lift
Their fronded palms in air,
But this I know, I cannot drift
Beyond His love and care.
—From a sermon by George W. Truett,
published by Erdmans Publishing Company

In every age there are people who triumph over their trials by having the right attitude. They have learned to trust in God and to make the best of their place in life. Others never seem to learn that they are making themselves and others miserable by having a bad attitude. We all need to look up, to trust in God, and to enjoy His blessings.

November 7
The Prayer Life of Jesus

"And in the morning, rising up a great while before day, he went out, and departed into a solitary place, and there prayed" (Mark 1:35).

Jesus often went to secluded places to escape the multitudes and pray. He prayed in the mountains. He prayed in the wilderness. He prayed in solitary places, He prayed in the Garden of Gethsemane, and He prayed on the cross. His prayer life kept Him in constant contact with the Father.

Jesus taught that men ought always to pray (Luke 18:1). We need to form regular habits of prayer. We are in a world that is filled with trials and heartaches. There are many things that we cannot control, and without the inner strength that God gives us when we pray, we can easily be overwhelmed.

November 8
Praise in the Morning

"But I will sing of thy power; yea, I will sing aloud

of thy mercy in the morning: for thou hast been my defence and refuge in the day of my trouble" (Psa. 59:16).

Singing praises to God in the morning will help us through the day. Singing praises can put joy in the heart, a light in the face, and a spring in the step. Singing God's praises can give us victory over problems, and help us be a blessing to others.

The following poem, often quoted by the late Dr. Fred Garland, tells how we should start the day.

> I met God in the morning
> When my day was at its best,
> And His presence came like sunrise,
> Like a glory in my breast.
> All day long the presence lingered,
> All day long He stayed with me,
> And we sailed in perfect calmness
> O'er a very troubled sea.
> So I think I know the secret,
> Learned from many a troubled way:
> You must seek Him in the morning
> If you want Him through the day!
> —Anonymous

November 9
Storms Build Faith

"And the same day, when the even was come, he saith unto them, Let us pass over unto the other side" (Mark 4:35).

Jesus knew that night was approaching and that a storm was brewing, yet He told His disciples to get in a ship and set sail for the other side of the Sea of Galilee.

The disciples dismissed the crowd that had

thronged them and their Master all day and boarded the ship. Weary from the day of ministering, Jesus went to the back of the ship and fell asleep (Matt. 8:23-24).

The disciples thrust away from the shore and started across the sea, but as they sailed a violent storm arose. Mountainous waves spilled into the ship, and it was in danger of capsizing.

The frightened disciples went to Jesus and awoke Him, crying, *"Master, carest thou not that we perish?"* Jesus calmly arose and rebuked the storm, and there followed a great calm.

The disciples would never have known the power of the Lord to control things when they get out of hand if He had not led them into the storm. Today our Lord often lets us go through storms to strengthen our faith. We do not learn faith when the sun is shining and the sea is calm. It is going through storms that build our faith.

November 10

Faithful Unto Death

". . . be thou faithful unto death, and I will give thee a crown of life" (Rev. 2:10).

The admonition of our text is taken from the letter Jesus dictated to John to be sent to the church at Smyrna. The letter speaks of persecution and martyrdom. Then comes the promise of a crown of life for those who are faithful unto death.

One shudders at the thought of being cruelly put to death for being a Christian. And one may wonder, "Would I have the courage to die for my faith?" If that test should ever come, many, perhaps most Christians would have the courage to die for Christ. However, many of the same people find it difficult to be faithful in His service day after day. Dying for Christ would be one brief, heroic act; living for Christ is a day to day experience that lasts for a lifetime.

An elderly man who had lost most of his hearing continued to attend church regularly, though he could not understand much of the singing or the preaching. When asked why he continued to attend church in spite of being unable to hear, he replied, "I want people to know whose side I'm on." That was being faithful.

November 11
Believe and Give Glory

"He (Abraham) *staggered not at the promise of God through unbelief; but was strong in faith, giving glory to God"* (Rom. 4:20).

Abraham believed the promises that God had made to him, and he staggered not while waiting for God to fulfill them. He even gave glory to God while he waited.

God does not always answer our prayers at once. Instead He moves with measured tread. He takes a springtime to paint the blush upon the cheeks of the flowers, and He uses a summer and a fall to bring the crops we plant to harvest. It is our part to till, to sow, to cultivate, and to wait for the harvest. It is God's part to send the sunshine and the rain that makes the harvest possible.

So it is in the spiritual realm. When we sow without prayer, we are likely to have a barren harvest. When we sow with prayer, faith, godly living, and service we reap a bountiful harvest.

In our times of prayer and meditation we should praise God for blessings we have not yet received.

We can be assured that, if we faint not in due time we shall reap (Gal. 6:9).

November 12
Encouragement to Pray

"Elias was a man subject to like passions as we are, and he prayed earnestly . . . And he prayed again . . ." (James 5:17,18).

Elijah was human. He had weaknesses just as we do. He became frightened and ran when Queen Jezebel threatened to kill him. He lay under a juniper tree, discouraged, and wished that he might die, yet God loved him and cared for him. Despite his weakness, God heard and answered his prayers.

The key phrase of our text is: *"He prayed again."* It is not enough to pray one time. We must pray again and again. You may wonder why we should pray when God knows what we need before we ask.

God does not want us to only pray occasionally, like a boy away from home who seldom writes to his mother. God wants us to stay in touch. We are not to treat God like a coin machine that we put a coin in and get something in return without caring what the machine is like or what happens to it. Nor are we to treat God like a spare tire that we only use in an emergency. God is a living being. He wants our love and our trust, and He wants us to keep in touch with Him.

November 13
Cause For Joy

"Then was our mouth filled with laughter, and our tongue with singing . . ." (Psa. 126:2).

The children of Israel had cause for joy. They had been in bondage in far-off Babylon. Now they were free, and they were going home. In Babylon they hanged their harps upon the willow tree and refused to sing, but now their mouths were filled with singing. They were free; they were going home, and they were laughing and singing.

We too were once in bondage. We were slaves of Satan, and there was little cause in our lives for singing. But when Jesus saved us, He set us free. He made us children of God, and we are now on our way to Heaven.

It did not matter to the Israelites that they had a long journey ahead of them, that they had to travel through desert country beneath a burning sun; they were happy to be going home. We also experience hardships in the journey of life, but we should never let them keep us from singing songs of victory.

November 14
The Place of Blessings

"So Naomi returned, and Ruth the Moabitess, her daughter in law, with her . . . and they came to Bethlehem in the beginning of barley harvest" (Ruth 1:22).

Bethlehem means the place of bread. Barley harvest means a time of plenty.

Ten years earlier Naomi had left Bethlehem and gone to the heathen country of Moab with her husband and their two sons. In Moab they had suffered. They had lost their inheritance, and Naomi's husband and her two sons had died.

Naomi finally realized that she was paying for her backsliding. After she returned to Bethlehem, she said, *"I went out full, and the Lord hath brought me home again empty . . ."* (Ruth 1:21).

While still in Moab Naomi heard that God had blessed His people. Perhaps she thought God would never bless her again, but there was nothing left for her in Moab, so she decided to go home, and her daughter-in-law, Ruth, went with her.

They arrived in Bethlehem at the beginning of barley harvest. That was a time of blessings for all, but it was a time of special blessings for Naomi and Ruth. Soon Ruth was gleaning in the harvest field of the wealthy Boaz. He saw Ruth, inquired who she was, and commanded that hands-full of barley be dropped on purpose for her. That night she carried home a bounty to her mother-in-law, and in time she was married to Boaz. She became the ancestress of King David and of Christ.

We learn from this Bible account that God will judge us if we get out of His will, and that He will bless us when we are in His will. We should learn to stay in God's appointed place and serve Him with joy. That is the place of blessings.

November 15
The Blessed Nation

"Blessed is the nation whose God is the Lord..." (Psa. 33:12).

During the reign of Queen Victoria a Zulu king visited her in England. The queen showed the Zulu king the great buildings and treasures of England, and she told him that her country controlled a territory so vast that the sun never set upon it.

When they returned to the palace, the queen sat on her throne, and the Zulu king stood before her with his hands crossed on his spear.

"White Queen, you have shown me impossible things," he said. "My people will not believe me when I tell them, but there is one word I want to take back with me. What is the secret of your power?"

The queen stepped from her throne, humbly picked up a Bible from a small table, and reverently lifted it before the black warrior. "This book contains within its pages the secret of England's greatness," she told him.

Since that time England has drifted from the foundation of which Queen Victoria spoke, and it is no longer the great nation that it was in her day.

America was founded upon the same foundation that made England great, but America has also drifted. Unless we in America return to God, we can no longer claim His protection and blessings. We can only return to God one person at a time. It is time for each of us to come into God's presence, confess our shortcomings, seek His blessings, and walk humbly before Him.

November 16
Being Faithful Always

"Therefore, my beloved brethren, be ye stedfast, unmoveable, always abounding in the work of the Lord . . ." (1 Cor. 15:58).

The following is a paraphrase of an article by an unknown author.

People came from far and wide to see a magnificent new church building. They commented on its many beautiful appointments, but a little nail on the roof got no attention at all. Hurt and jealous, the nail started feeling sorry for itself. Finally it decided that nobody would miss it if it quit, so it let go its hold on a shingle, slid down the roof and fell in the mud.

That night there was a high wind and a hard rain. The loose shingle blew off and the roof started leaking. Water soaked the plaster, streaked the walls, and stained the beautiful murals. Plaster started falling and ruined the beautiful carpet. The pulpit Bible was soaked and ruined. The nail that had quit was lost in the mud where it rusted away. It never again served a useful purpose.

Some of God's people serve in insignificant ways, but their service is important. None of us can afford to quit the cause of Christ. We should be faithful for His sake or for the sake of our own testimony.

November 17
Preparing for Service

"Study to shew thyself approved unto God, a workman that needeth not to be ashamed . . ." (2 Tim. 2:15).

When I was a young pastor, I learned a great lesson from a crippled man who was affectionately called "Hopsy" by all who knew him. Hopsy was a poor man with little education, but he lived for God, and he was a student of the Bible. I taught the men's Sunday school class, and Hopsy was in my class.

One Sunday during the lesson Hopsy asked a question that I could not answer. That embarrassed me and made me feel humiliated. On the spot I decided that I would study the Bible until I could answer most any question about its teachings.

How well I have succeeded I will leave to others to decide, but I am certainly not as easily embarrassed now as I was that day. I share this testimony to encourage others to make a lifelong study of God's Word. Paul reminded Timothy that he had known the Scriptures from his childhood, and added that the Scriptures were able to make him wise unto salvation (2 Tim. 3:15).

One who has little education but has a good understanding of the Bible cannot be considered uneducated, and one who has a degree in education but has no knowledge of the Bible is not really educated.

November 18

The Wonderful Name

". . . thou shalt call his name JESUS: for he shall save his people from their sins" (Matt. 1:21).

In all of human history there has never been another name that has so changed the world as the name of Jesus. The name, Jesus, speaks of the virgin birth in the manger, of the mighty miracles that Jesus performed, of His agony in Gethsemane, of the cross upon which He died, and of the empty tomb from which He arose.

The letters of His name are usually stamped with printers's ink, but it is easy to imagine that the light of the star of Bethlehem cast shadows in the straw of the manger that spelled the name of Jesus. Or we can imagine that His name was formed in the grain of His wooden cross. We can almost see the letters of His name twisted and distorted in the thorns of the crown He wore, and, while He was hanging on the cross the blood that dripped from His toes could have formed His name in blood.

His name is a wonderful name. His name is above every name, for He is the eternal Saviour, High Priest, and soon coming Lord. He was named in Heaven before Mary ever called Him Jesus, and we can almost imagine His name emblazoned on a sapphire cloud at the time of His Second Coming. His name, Jesus, is the most wonderful name.

November 19

Praying Always

". . . men ought always to pray, and not to faint"
(Luke 18:1).

We should pray until the Jordan rolls back and
we can walk dry-shod across it to the land of milk
and honey. We should pray until our walls of Jericho
bow low in submission. We should pray until the
manna of blessings falls from Heaven and the quails
from God's poultry yard drop at our feet. We should
pray until our Philippian jail shakes and quakes and
the doors that bind us fall off their hinges. We should
pray as Paul and Silas did until lost people cry, "What
must I do to be saved?"

We should pray, as Elijah did, until the thunder
rolls, the lightning flashes, and the rain of blessings
falls. We should pray until our Red Sea parts and a
cloud of fire leads us across it to victory. We should
pray until a Mississippi of blessing flows into our
hearts and the fires of Pentecost fall and revival
comes. We should pray until horses of fire pull a
chariot of fire up to our dwelling and we get on board
with Gabriel and Michael and fly away past worlds
of fire to the gates of light and angels sing, *"Lift
your heads, O ye gates; even lift them up, ye everlasting doors; and the King of glory shall come in"*
(Psa. 24:9). Ours is the victory through prayer.

November 20

Getting Back Lost Joy

"Restore unto me the joy of thy salvation . . ."
(Psa. 51:12).

David had sinned, and because of his sin he had
lost the joy of his salvation. Deeply convicted, he

repented, and in his prayer of repentance he prayed that the joy of his salvation would be restored. Any sin, even so-called small sins, can rob us of our joy. Or we can lose our joy when we drift and become spiritually cold. In either case we need to return to God. It is our part to confess our sins. It is God's part to forgive our sins and restore our joy.

We can keep our joy by walking in constant fellowship with the Lord. The poem below tells what it is like to wander away from the Lord then to return.

I Have Returned

Days without number I wandered away,
Far from the Lord and the straight, narrow way.
Days without number He would not let go
Until I returned to the One who loved so.
Now I have returned like a sheep to the fold,
And I have found blessings that I cannot hold.
The pastures are green, and the waters are still
Since I have returned to live in God's will.

—Louis Arnold

November 21
A Place Prepared

". . . I go to prepare a place for you" (John 14:2).

Years ago, radio evangelist, Charles Fuller, announced that on the next Sunday broadcast he would preach on Heaven. That week he received a most interesting letter from a very sick, elderly man. The letter follows in part.

"I am interested in that Land because I have held a clear title to a bit of property there for over 55 years. I did not buy it, but the Donor purchased it at a tremendous sacrifice. It is not a vacant lot. For more than half a century I have been sending materials out of which the greatest Architect and Builder in the universe has been building a home for me.

"I cannot reach my home in that city of gold without passing through the dark valley of shadows. I am not afraid because the best friend I ever had went through that valley long ago and drove away its gloom. I hold His promise in printed form, never to forsake me or leave me alone. He will be with me when I walk through the valley of shadows, and I shall not lose my way." Thank God that He has prepared a place for a prepared people.

November 22

Paul's Conflicting Desires

"For I am in a strait betwixt two, having a desire to depart, and to be with Christ; which is far better" (Phil. 1:23).

After many trials, the Apostle Paul is in prison in Rome, and he appears to have grown homesick for Heaven. In verse 21 he wrote, *". . . to die is gain."* In Philippians 1:22 he wrote of his work and ended by saying, *". . . what I shall choose I wot not."* Then he laments *"For I am in a strait betwixt two . . . "* It appears that Paul hardly knew whether he wanted to live or die. Of one thing he was certain, there is a life after death.

Throughout the long history of the world people of every race and culture have believed in life beyond the grave. The desire for life in the hereafter is a universally inborn instinct.

There are examples of inborn instinct in many of the creatures God has created. For example, monarch butterflies, hatched east of the Rockies, migrate from Central Mexico to Canada. They lay their eggs on milkweeds along the way. Their young, hatched miles from their native home in Mexico, go back there by instinct to spend the winter. Just as their inborn desire has a fulfillment, so will ours.

One day every saved person will migrate to a far better land than Mexico or any other place on earth. Like Paul, we sometimes grow homesick for that better country.

November 23
We Need Never Be Alone

"*. . . I will be with him in trouble; I will deliver him, and honour him*" (Psa. 91:15).

In verse 1 of the 91st Psalm we read, "*He that dwelleth in the secret place of the most High shall abide under the shadow of the Almighty.*"

Through centuries untold, devout Christians have pillowed their heads upon the promises of God, and in times of trouble, they have found God nearer than at other times.

Comforting also is the promise, "*I will deliver him.*" Who can count the times when God has answered prayer and delivered them when there seemed no solution to a problem? God is always near, and that means we are never alone.

> Wherever the clouds of sorrow roll,
> And trials overwhelm the mind—
> When faint with grief, thy wearied soul
> No joy on earth can find,
> Then lift thy voice to God on high;
> Dry away thy trembling tear,
> And hush the low, complaining sigh.
> "Fear not, thy God is nigh."
>   —Author unknown

November 24

Redemption's Price

"When Jesus therefore had received the vinegar, he said, It is finished: and he bowed his head, and gave up the ghost" (John 19:30).

When Jesus said, *"It is finished,"* perhaps an angel, hovering near the cross, winged his way to the gate of pearl and shouted for all to hear, *"It is finished!"* Inside the city, along Glory Street and Hallelujah Boulevard, on King Avenue and Apostles Plaza, they must have shouted one to another, *"It is finished! It is finished!"*

The saints of the Old Testament era, yet in Paradise, must have heard and shouted one to another, *"It is finished!"*

Perhaps the demons heard and realized that their supposed victory had turned into defeat, and they must have crawled away whimpering, "Alas, it is finished!"

The final payment had been made on the debt of sin. Redemption's plan was complete. Today we can rejoice that Jesus paid for our redemption, and we can echo with boundless joy, "It is finished! It is finished."

November 25

The All Sufficient Gospel

"For I am not ashamed of the gospel of Christ: for it is the power of God unto salvation to every one that believeth . . ." (Rom. 1:16).

Years ago, near Florence, Alabama, they built Wilson Dam. For years it was the largest dam in the world, and it had the largest turbine in the world. Sixty feet down under the water there was a huge dynamo able to produce enough electrical power for all the cities up and down the Tennessee Valley.

One day a preacher was being shown through the facility, and the guide said, "This is the greatest source of power on earth."

"Not so," the preacher said. "The Gospel is the greatest source of power on earth." What he said is true. No other power can save the lost from sin and transform their lives .

An old Baptist preacher said of the Gospel, "When I was thirty years old I said, 'Nothing is better than the Gospel.' When I was forty, I said, 'Nothing is as good as the Gospel.' When I was fifty, I said, 'There is nothing to be compared to the Gospel. When I was sixty, I said, 'There is nothing but the Gospel.' " All of what he said is true, for the Gospel is the good news that sinners can be saved by receiving Jesus as Lord and Saviour.

November 26
Morning Always Comes

"But when the morning was now come, Jesus stood on the shore: but the disciples knew not that it was Jesus" (John 21:4).

It had been a long night for Peter and the six disciples who were with him. The earthly ministry of Jesus had ended, and they did not understand what the future held. So they had returned to fishing. They had fished all night and caught nothing. When morning finally came, they saw Jesus standing on the shore, but they did not recognize Him.

Contrast the morning with the night. Night is the time of suffering. It is often asked concerning the sick, "Did he or she have a good night?" Night is also the time of worry. We often take our worries to bed with us and spend a restless night. This we should not do, for there never was a sunset that was not followed by a sunrise.

Like the disciples, we often fail to recognize the Lord when He comes to us. We should remember that eternal morning will come, and Jesus will be with us in the new day. We will be able to walk in His light, for He is the Light, and we will be able to put our troubles behind us, place our hand in His hand, and walk with Him. Thank God that sunrise always comes.

November 27
Christ Is All

> ". . . *but Christ is all . .*" (Col. 3:11).

Jesus Christ is woven through the tapestry of the Word of God like a golden thread. In the first book of the Bible, He is the seed of woman. In the last book of the Bible He is the Alpha and Omega.

He is pictured in the types, in the Pentateuch, in the Poetry, and in the Prophets. The Gospels are about Him, and He is prominent in the Acts of the Apostles, the Epistles, and The Revelation. The Bible tells of His birth, of His life, of His miracles, of His teachings, of His death, of His burial, of His resurrection, and of His Second Coming.

When we receive Jesus as Saviour, He becomes our friend, our High Priest, our deliverer, and our soon coming Lord. Christ is all in Heaven, and He should be our all on earth. We should love Him, walk with Him, pray to Him, worship Him, and be ready to meet Him when He comes again.

November 28
Our Shelter in Time of Storm

> "*The LORD is my rock, and my fortress, and my deliverer; my God, my strength, in whom I will trust . . .*" (Psa. 18:2).

In this Psalm David rejoiced and gave praise that the Lord had given him victory over his enemies. He had reason to testify, *"The LORD is my rock, and my fortress . . ."*

When there is a storm at sea, the winds often drive mighty waves against the face of a cliff. The waves appear strong enough to shatter the cliff, but they fall back, broken into foam. The waves roar and charge again, but in vain. The cliff remains unharmed. In like manner the devil attacks the children of God.

His roar is often loud enough to make us tremble. When that happens we should remember that God is our rock and our fortress. He can give us victory over the devil and all his demons. He can make them creep away defeated, while angels strike their harps of gold and sing, "All hail! the victory has been won." The victory is ours through the Lord Jesus Christ.

November 29
Victory over the Fear of Death

"And deliver them who through fear of death were all their lifetime subject to bondage" (Heb. 2:15).

Job feared death and asked if man would live again after dying (Job 14:14). Then God gave him faith to believe that after death he would live again. We can almost hear him shout, *". . . yet in my flesh shall I see God"* (Job 19:26).

God created man with a longing in his heart that reaches beyond the narrow confines of this little life. God gave us an unquenchable longing for life beyond this short voyage.

Paul wrote that if we only have hope in this life, *"we are of all men most miserable."* Then he hastened to add, *"But now is Christ risen"* (1 Cor. 15:19-20).

Because Christ lives, we shall live also. Death is

only a transition. Death is a promotion. Death is a door into the spirit world. Death is graduation time.

Saved loved ones who have gone from us have gone to a better country. When our time comes for us to go, we will also go to that better country. In that fair Land we will see face to face, and we will know as we are known. We can cry with Paul, *"O death, where is thy sting? O grave, where is thy victory?"* (1 Cor. 15:55).

November 30

Our Father's Care

". . . God feedeth them (the ravens)*: how much more are ye better than the fowls?"* (Luke 12:24).

A man who was traveling on a luxury cruise went several days without going to the dining table. Finally someone remarked that he had not seen him at the table.

"I'm short of money, so I brought some cheese and crackers aboard to eat on the trip," he explained.

"But your meals were included in the fare you paid," he was told. After that he gladly went to the dining table for his meals. Likewise many of God's children are living on the devil's cheese and crackers instead of enjoying the bounty God has provided for them.

God wants us to know that we are of more value than ravens, and that He will provide for us. Instead of fretting and worrying, we can travel first class.

Devotions for December

December 1
We Have Work to Do

"For the Son of man is as a man taking a far journey, who left his house, and gave authority to his servants, and to every man his work . . ." (Mark 13:34).

The great preacher, Henry Ward Beecher, expressed appreciation for a horse he was hiring, and the livery-man told him that the horse would work anywhere and would do all that any horse could do. Beecher regarded the horse with greater appreciation. Then he said, "I wish he were a member of my church."

We can take a lesson from the horse that so impressed Dr. Beecher. The horse did not fret because he could not do more, but he was faithful in doing what he could do.

God has given each of us work to do. We do not all have the same talents, so we cannot all do the same work. God knows our abilities, and He gives us tasks that we can perform. We should not complain and whimper because we would rather have the task God has assigned to someone else. Even if what we are doing seems small we should be faithful in doing it. Being faithful in small tasks often opens the door to greater opportunities.

If we are faithful in doing what we can in the

Lord's service, one day we will hear Him say, *". . . Well done, good and faithful servant; thou hast been faithful over a few things, I will make thee ruler over many things: enter thou into the joy of thy lord"* (Matt. 25:23).

December 2

The Necessity of a Vision

"Where there is no vision, the people perish . . ." (Prov. 29:18).

In the chapter six of Isaiah we have a record of the prophet's heavenly vision. In verse one he tells of seeing the Lord on a throne, high and lifted up. In verses two and three he tells of seeing seraphims and of hearing them cry one to another *" . . . Holy, holy, holy, is the LORD of hosts: the whole earth is full of his glory."* In verse five he tells of his vision of himself, and of the people around him.

What a contrast. He saw the Lord high, and holy, and he saw himself and his neighbors as men of unclean lips. After his visions and the Lord's call for someone to go for Him, Isaiah was ready to say, *" . . . Here am I; send me."*

One cold winter night, a beggar, who was thought to be mentally deranged, was saved in a Chicago mission. Within three years he wore out three Bibles. A newspaper reporter found him on his knees with an open Bible before him and asked him to read from the Bible. After hearing the man read, the reporter wrote that he had never heard anyone read the Bible as the converted beggar did. He asked him how was able to read the Bible with such power. The convert replied, "I have seen Jesus."

The beggar had also seen himself and repented.

It is most likely that he also saw the need of others. We all need the threefold vision, a vision of the glory of God, a vision of our need, and a vision of the needs of others.

December 3
God Is Eternal

"I am Alpha and Omega, the beginning and the ending, saith the Lord, which is, and which was, and which is to come, the Almighty" (Rev. 1:8).

Before the morning stars sang together, before the first rays of cosmic light pierced the gloom, before the smallest world was born, before the first ocean rocked in its primal bed, before the breath of life quivered in the nostrils of the first man, there was God, and Jesus was with Him.

Eternity never had a beginning, and it will never have an end. Isaiah tells us that God dwells in eternity (Isa. 57:15). That means that God never had a beginning, and He will never have an end. Likewise, Jesus never had a beginning, and He will never have an end.

When we are born-again, Jesus gives us eternal life. We had a beginning, but we will never have an end. Physical life ends, but spiritual life does not. In the resurrection we will receive bodies that will never die. Let us rejoice that our Saviour has given us eternal life and that we will be with Him forever in the Land where there is no death.

December 4
The Hiding Place

"He that dwelleth in the secret place of the most High shall abide under the shadow of the Almighty" (Psa. 91:1).

David often hid in secret places in the mountains when Saul was trying to kill him. There was always the possibility that Saul would find him in some hiding place, so he looked for a better hiding place and found it in the most High God. By faith he could abide under the shadow of the Almighty, and there would be no more moving and looking for a better hiding place.

Like David, we have an enemy. The devil is trying to destroy us. There is no earthly hiding place where we can escape from him, but, like David, we have a shelter in the most High, and we can abide under His shadow.

In verses one and two of this Psalm, God is called by four names. He is called the Most High, the Almighty, Lord, and God. There is no mistaking who is our shelter and protector. We have an abiding place in the Most High. That is where we belong. We are not simply to visit God when we are in trouble. We are to abide with Him every day.

December 5
The Walk of Faith

"For we walk by faith, not by sight" (2 Cor. 5:7).

Faith is the power line that makes contact with God. Faith is the Jacob's ladder that reaches from earth to Heaven. Faith brought manna from Heaven, quails from the wilderness, water from a rock, and money from a fish's mouth. Faith appropriates salvation for the sinner. Faith cashes the promises of God for the Christian. Faith is a physician for the sick, and a pillow for the head of the dying.

The Word of God is a faith builder (Rom. 10:17). Faith is also built by experience. A missionary told an African convert that he could walk across rivers on ice that froze in his homeland in the winter. The convert could hardly believe what the missionary told him.

Later the missionary came home on furlough and brought the convert home with him. It was wintertime, and the missionary took his convert to the river and showed him that it was frozen over. The convert was convinced that ice did indeed form on the river when it was cold. The missionary walked out on the ice and jumped up and down. That convinced the convert that the ice would support him, and he walked out on the ice with the missionary. What he had seen gave him faith to walk on the ice. Just so, things we see God do in answer to prayer builds our faith.

December 6
Continuing in the Lord

". . . for your goodness is as a morning cloud, and as the early dew it goeth away" (Hos. 6:4).

The words of our text were addressed to Ephraim and Judah, but they can well be addressed to many Christians today.

In the mountains dew collects on the grass during the night, and fog rises from the valleys in the early morning, but neither of them lasts. When the sun rises above the mountains the fog soon dissipates and the dew dries. All too often Christians fall by the wayside like the disappearing fog and drying morning dew.

Becoming a Christian is the beginning of a life-long journey. Being born-again is like a baby being born into the world. A baby must be fed and cared for, and it must grow and learn on its way to adulthood. When we are born into the family of God we also need to learn and grow.

Our goodness should never go away like a morning cloud. We are supposed to continue in the Lord and grow in grace. In order to grow, we need to attend a good Bible-preaching church where we can hear the preaching of God's Word. We need to read the Bible and pray daily, and we need to be involved in the Lord's work. These things can be a blessing, not a burden. The Lord's yoke is easy, and His burden is light (Matt. 11:30). Continuing in His service will bring joy and make us a blessing to others.

December 7

The Blessing of Giving

"Give, and it shall be given unto you; good measure, pressed down, and shaken together, and running over, shall men give into your bosom . . ." (Luke 6:38).

We are not to give in order to get a blessing; we are to give in order to be a blessing. When we give we not only bless others, we get blessed ourselves.

Someone made up a parable about a brook and a pool. Said the pool to the brook, "The way you're running, you're going to run dry. I'm going to horde my water for I know a summer drought is coming." The brook murmured happily and kept on flowing.

When the summer drought came, the pool became stagnate, and it became infested with mosquitoes and malaria. Birds did not drink from it, nor did man or any passing animal stop to drink.

The brook continued to flow, and its water remained clear and fresh. Flowers blossomed along its banks, and birds sang in the trees above it. It gave its water freely to all that would stop and drink, and its giving did not cause it to dry up or slow its journey.

The Sea of Galilee and the Dead Sea are also examples of this principle. The Jordan River flows into the Sea of Galilee, flows through it and continues its journey down the valley. The Sea of Galilee gives as much water as it receives, and it is beautiful and alive. Ships ply its waters, and fishermen fill their nets with fish from it.

The Jordan reaches the Dead Sea and flows into it, but it does not flow out of it. The Dead Sea hordes its water. That is why it is dead. There are no fish living in the Dead Sea, and no living creature stops to drink from it. The lesson is clear. We must give if we are to receive of the Father's bounty. Our text says, *"Give, and it shall be given unto you . . ."*

December 8
The Great Divide

". . . choose you this day whom ye will serve . . ." (Josh. 24:15).

Everyone is either serving God or the devil, and the one they choose to serve determines their eternal destiny. In nature there is a powerful illustration of the consequences of choice.

Nine hundred and fifty miles West of Winnipeg, Canada, a railroad runs through a little city that is five thousand feet above sea level. A stream, visible from passing trains, runs north to a point that is called, "The Great Divide." There the stream seems to hesitate as if uncertain which way to go. Then it divides, and part of it flows west to the Pacific Ocean, and part of it flows east to the Atlantic. That simple division determines the destination of both parts of the water in the stream.

Jesus is the great divide for the human race. Those

who receive Him travel the upward road to Heaven. Those who reject Him continue downward to the destination of the unsaved. There is a time when the water at "The Great Divide" is forced to divide, but people are not forced to receive or reject Jesus. They have a choice, and that choice determines their eternal destination.

All have the choice to make, and that choice will determine where they will spend eternity. Those who receive Jesus have the privilege of serving Him every day. He will be their friend, and He will walk with them through the journey of life and into eternity.

December 9
A Wake-Up Call

"The backslider in heart shall be filled with his own ways: and a good man shall be satisfied from himself" (Prov. 14:14).

One can become backslidden in heart without realizing it. It happens gradually, because of neglect of prayer, Bible reading, church attendance, and being active in the Lord's work. When it does happen, one is filled with his own ways and no longer pursues the way of the Lord's direction. The joy of salvation is lost. So is the feeling of victory and well-being.

On the other hand, living in the will of God brings peace of mind. Jesus spoke of a well of water within the believer that springs up into everlasting life (John 4:14). That well of water gives satisfaction within and enables us to be a blessing to others.

When there is the slightest evidence of coldness of heart, we should confess to the Lord and ask Him to forgive us and restore us. Then we should walk in His will and share the blessings and the joy He gives us with others.

December 10

Precious Trials

". . . when he hath tried me, I shall come forth as gold" (Job 23:10).

We all have trials. A boat can be in the water without getting wet as easily as a person can be in the world without trials. Because sin is in the world, trouble is in the world, and trials come to everyone.

We do not enjoy trials, but they are necessary to our spiritual growth. If a stone in the hands of a sculptor had a voice, it would surely cry out as hammers and chisels chip and cut piece after piece from it. But that is the only way the stone can be fashioned into the thing of beauty the sculptor has in mind. Just so, God uses trials to mold us.

The refiner of gold keeps the ore over intense heat until he can see his face reflected in its molten surface. In like manner God uses our trials to bring us to the place where we reflect His image.

A songwriter of long ago put it well in the following words:

> When through fiery trials thy pathway shall lie,
> My grace, all sufficient, shall be thy supply;
> The flames shall not hurt thee, I only design
> Thy dross to consume, and thy gold to refine.

December 11

Strength for the Journey

". . . the joy of the LORD is your strength" (Neh. 8:10).

The joy of the Lord is the birthright of every Christian. Some experience joy from the moment they are converted; others do not, but that should not cause them concern. Instead, they should get busy working for the Lord. They will soon find that being active in the work of the Lord will give them joy. Noise does not pull a wagon, but a wagon in motion does produce noise. A Christian in motion for the Lord will soon begin to experience joy.

Some do not want to appear joyful. They think that a pious, non-joyful demeanor is a sign of spirituality. Others lose their joy when they follow the Lord afar off. Still others lose their joy when they venture into sin. That is what happened to King David when he sinned. God convicted him of his sin, and he prayed for the Lord to forgive him and to restore the joy of his salvation.

Joyful Christians are strong Christians. They are strong because they are close to the Lord. Their joy is not a result of conditions. They are joyful even in times of disappointment or sorrow. The Lord is nearer to us when we are experiencing trouble or sorrow than at any other time. Even in these times, *" . . . the joy of the Lord is your strength."*

December 12

Let Us Rejoice

"FINALLY, my brethren, rejoice in the Lord . . ." (Phil. 3:1).

Paul practiced what he preached. The epistle of Philippians was written in a prison cell, yet it was his most joyful, victorious epistle. In it he used the words joy and rejoice 19 times.

In chapter 3 Paul wrote, *"Finally, my brethren,"* but that was not his final word on the subject. In chapter 4 he wrote, *"Rejoice in the Lord alway: and again I say, Rejoice"* (Phil. 4:4).

Joyful Christians are filled with thankfulness and praise. Joy shows in their countenances. Their very appearance is a testimony. Gloomy Christians are poor advertisements for the Lord. It is not surprising that the unsaved say of them, "If that is Christianity, I want no part of it."

The story goes: There was a Christian lady who was a chronic complainer. When someone asked why she was always talking about her troubles, she answered, "When the Lord gives me tribulations, I think I have a right to 'tribulate.'"

That is not the way Christians should behave. We should rejoice in the Lord in good weather and in foul weather. We should rejoice when all goes well, and we should rejoice when things go against us. Our days will be brighter and things go better when we rejoice in the Lord. Further, our testimony is stronger when we rejoice. A long face is a poor testimony.

December 13
Importance of Proper Thinking

". . . think on these things" (Phil. 4:8).

Thoughts control our behavior and our attitude. If we think we are in danger we immediately spring into action. When someone tells us we look great, that lifts our spirits. If they tell us that we do not look well, we start feeling down.

Some friends of the postmaster in a small Kentucky town decided to play a trick on him. One of them went to the post office and asked if he was feeling well. He assured his friend that he was, but his spirits dropped. Another friend went by and asked the same question. This time he started feeling a bit under the weather. Other friends dropped by and told him that he did not look well, and he started feeling really ill. He soon went home and went to bed. His thoughts had made him really sick.

Thinking the wrong thoughts can lead one into sin, for temptation begins in the mind. Thinking the right thoughts can help us grow in the Lord. In the first part of our text Paul tells us to think on the following things, "*. . . whatsoever things are true, whatsoever things are honest, whatsoever things are just, whatsoever things are pure, whatsoever things are lovely, whatsoever things are of good report.*" Such thoughts do not lead one into sin. Neither do they cause discouragement or lead to defeat. When we think right, believe right, and act right, we will be right. That will be pleasing to God, and it will improve our quality of life.

December 14
The Sure Foundation

"*. . . Behold, I lay in Zion for a foundation a stone, a tried stone, a precious corner stone, a sure foundation . . .*" (Isa. 28:16).

Jesus is the sure foundation. In 1 Corinthians 3:11 Paul tells us that Jesus is the foundation, and in Acts 4:11 Peter said that He is the head of the corner. That foundation will never pass away.

When the stars are wrung from their sockets and fall like glowing balls of fire, when this blood-soaked, sin-blackened world is falling apart in the throws of its last agony, when it blazes with its last volcano and shakes with its last earthquake, when its ashes are blown away in the last tornado, the foundation of Jesus Christ will abide.

Other foundations fail. Good works, religion, penance, baptism, and church membership all fail if we are not built upon the foundation of Jesus Christ. He is the only Saviour. *"Neither is there salvation in any other: for there is none other name under heaven given among men, whereby we must be saved"* (Acts 4:12).

He is the all-sufficient Saviour. All who receive Him are saved. All who reject Him are lost. He is the sure foundation of the saved. We have cause to rejoice in His service.

December 15

What to Do When Discouraged

"This poor man cried, and the LORD heard him, and saved him out of all his troubles" (Psa. 34:6).

According to a published sermon by C. A. Dixon, Florence Nightingale related a story she heard from sailors on her way to the Crimean War. The sailors told her that birds with black wings and blue breast often flew across the Black Sea in stormy weather. After reaching land, they roosted in cypress trees, and on dark nights their doleful cries mingled with the sighing of the wind in the trees. The Moslems thought the spirits of the lost dwelt in the birds and their cries were the wailing of lost spirits.

Such birds, with black wings and blue breasts, sometimes fly into our lives, bringing sadness, heaviness, and discouragement. Without knowing why, we have the blues.

When that happens, what are we to do? We are to do precisely what the writer of our text did. He saw himself as a poor man in trouble. He called upon the Lord, then rejoiced that the Lord had heard him and delivered him out of all his troubles.

December 16
How Great Thou Art

"For the invisible things of him from the creation of the world are clearly seen . . ." (Rom. 1:20).

We should remember God's greatness and take time to worship Him. All about us are evidences of His power, His love, and His care. Heathen in the jungle read the book of nature and know that there is a God. I too have read that book and know that there is a God.

I have walked across a dew-drenched meadow in the morning and watched the rising sun turn dewdrops into a diamonds and have exulted, "How great Thou art." I have listened to birds singing from the treetops, melodies without printed music or a director of the winged orchestra. I have marveled at the music God has imprinted in their tiny brains, and I have cried, "How great Thou art." At the ending of day, I have watched the sun go down into the sea and turn the restless waves to liquid fire, and I have cried, "How great Thou art." I have watched the shining stars move across the heavens in their courses, and I have cried again, "How great Thou art."

I have marveled that God loves us and gave His Son to die for us, and I have cried, "How great Thou art."

We should rejoice every day in God's greatness and His love, and we should serve Him with hearts full of love.

December 17
Our Birthright

". . . I am come that they might have life, and that they might have it more abundantly" (John 10:10).

Jesus came to seek and to save the lost (Luke 19:10). He also came to give abundant life to all who receive Him as Saviour.

A cocoon, hanging from the limb of a tree, has life, but that life does not compare with the life it will have when it becomes a butterfly. There is no beauty in the cocoon, but the butterfly is a beautiful creature. A butterfly rides upon the wind and takes its food from the fairest flowers. That is a more abundant life, but it does not compare with the abundant life of those who are born-again.

Unsaved people have physical life. That is life in this world only, and the existence they will have in eternity is called the second death. Their life is not to be compared with the life that saved people have,

Saved people have spiritual life. That gives them more abundant life in this world, and they will have eternal life in the world to come. They are a new creation in this world, and in the world to come they will be like Jesus. The Holy Spirit indwells saved people in this world, and they already have the joy that only Jesus can give. Saved people have the privilege of prayer, and they can enjoy the blessings of the Lord. Best of all, they have the promise that they will never die.

December 18
Saved to Serve

"For we are his workmanship, created in Christ Jesus unto good works . . ." (Eph. 2:10).

We are not saved by good works; we are saved so we can perform good works. We are God's workmanship. He has given us a new nature. That new nature has the desire and the ability to serve Him. Unsaved people cannot perform works pleasing to God, for they are living in rebellion to Him. The Bible tells us that even the plowing of the wicked is sin (Prov. 21:4).

An eagle has the ability to soar in the clouds. It would be contrary to nature if an eagle spent its life in the chicken yard, walking and feeding with chickens. Just so, it is contrary to the new nature for Christians to live for the world.

Further, Christians should not sit on the sidelines. We should never be content to be bench-warmers in the game of life or drones in God's beehives. Working bees are the ones that make honey, and working Christians are the ones who get the job done for God.

December 19

Reason to Rejoice

"I will greatly rejoice in the LORD, my soul shall be joyful in my God . . ." (Isa. 61:10).

Rejoicing in the Lord is based upon a decision. We can decide to begin our day with prayer, worship, and praise. Making that decision will get the day started right, and we can have a good day all day long.

On the other hand, making the wrong decision can cause us to have a terrible day. We can decide to wallow in self-pity, harbor a grudge, or brood over a disappointment. We can spend the day growling, grumbling, and complaining. Having that kind of attitude will make us miserable and upset those around us.

At times we all have days that do not go well. When that happens we should start the day over. We should get alone, if possible, and spend time with the Lord. That usually lifts the burden and helps us to rejoice instead of complain.

December 20
Loving Others

"Herein is love, not that we loved God, but that he loved us, and sent his Son to be the propitiation for our sins. Beloved, if God so loved us, we ought also to love one another" (1 John 4:10-11).

It is amazing that God loved us when we were poor, unworthy, sinful mortals, and it is marvelous that He saved us by His grace when we had no merit of our own. Because God loved us and saved us, we ought to love others.

Our hearts are difficult to control. We cannot make ourselves love people who irritate us or misuse us by telling ourselves that we are going to love them. We could as easily generate light in a dark room by clapping our hands and jumping up and down as we can make ourselves love someone that we do not like. Yet, we are told in the Bible to love one another (John 13:34). We are even told that we are to love our enemies and pray for those who despitefully use us (Matt. 5:44).

God is love, so it is His nature to love, but that is not our nature. We can only love as we should when God gives us the ability. To have that ability, we must be yielded to God and filled with His Holy Spirit. The Bible tells us that, *". . . the love of God is shed abroad in our hearts by the Holy Ghost which is given unto us"* (Rom. 5:5). Only in this way can we love as we are loved.

December 21
The Power of Faith

"THEN Job answered the LORD, and said, I know that thou canst do every thing . . ." (Job 42:1-2).

Through the centuries men have wondered why Job had to go through such great trials. Job was not tried because he was sinful. God attested that he was the best man on earth. Job's problem was his fear.

When everything went wrong in Job's life, he confessed his fear. He said, *"For the thing which I greatly feared is come upon me, and that which I was afraid of is come unto me"* (Job 3:25).

Job feared that his children would not serve God, and he offered burnt offerings continually for them (Job 1:5). He hoped that by offering burnt offerings in their stead, they would be protected. Job was also afraid of dying. He even questioned if there would be life after death (Job 14:14). Apparently he was also afraid of losing his property, his health, and his standing with others.

In spite of all his trials, Job's faith finally triumphed. He became convinced that God could do anything. That enabled him to get his mind off of himself and to stop worrying. He started thinking of others and even started praying for his former friends who had now become his critics (Job 42:10). That was when God started blessing him.

God did not bless Job because of his fear. He blessed him because of his faith. God uses faith. Satan uses fear. Faith is stronger than fear. When Job exercised faith God blessed him.

December 22

What to Do When Trouble Comes

"Yet man is born unto trouble, as the sparks fly upward" (Job 5:7).

"LET not your heart be troubled: ye believe in God, believe also in me" (John 1 4:1).

In the journey of life, we all encounter trouble.

That is because trouble is in the world. Trouble is in the world because sin is in the world. We all face the problem of what to do when trouble comes our way.

Jesus tells us in two simple words what to do when trouble comes. He tells us to believe. We are to believe in God and believe in Jesus, our Saviour. Further, in the verses that follow our text, Jesus tells us that we are to believe in life after death, in a home of many mansions, and in His Second Coming. In short, we are to believe in God's great realities.

Faith is the antidote for trouble. Faith is the victory that overcomes the world. We have a problem when trouble gets into our hearts. Only faith can keep that from happening. Storms may sweep around us, but by faith we can sail serenely through them.

December 23

Behold the Man

". . . Pilate saith unto them, Behold the man!" (John 19:5).

An unknown author wrote, "More than two thousand years ago a man was born contrary to the laws of nature. He lived in poverty and was reared in obscurity. Only once, during His exile in childhood, did He cross the boundary of His native land. He possessed neither wealth nor influence. His relatives were unknown and without influence. He had neither training nor education.

"In infancy He startled a king. In childhood He puzzled doctors. In manhood He ruled the course of nature, walked upon tossing billows, and hushed the sea to sleep. He healed the multitudes without medicine and made no charge for His services.

"He never wrote a book, yet all the libraries in the world cannot contain the books that have been written about Him. He never wrote a song, yet He has furnished the theme for more songs than all the songwriters combined. He never founded a college, but all the schools put together cannot boast of having as many students. He never marshalled an army, drafted a soldier, or fired a gun, yet no general ever had more volunteers under His orders who made more rebels stack arms and surrender without a shot being fired.

"Time has spread 2000 years between His generation and the present, yet He lives. He stands upon the highest pinnacle of heavenly glory, proclaimed by God, acknowledged by angels, and adored by saints. He is the living Christ, the Lord of glory!"

——Edited and copied in part

December 24

The Prophets Proclaimed Him

"Therefore the Lord himself shall give you a sign; Behold, a virgin shall conceive, and bear a son, and shall call his name Immanuel" (Isa. 7:14).

"For unto us a child is born, unto us a son is given: and the government shall be upon his shoulder: and his name shall be called Wonderful, Counsellor, The mighty God, The everlasting Father, The Prince of Peace" (Isa. 9:6).

More than 700 years before the birth of Christ, Isaiah made several predictions concerning Him. He predicted that He would be born of a virgin, and that His miraculous birth would be a sign. The virgin birth is one of the ways we know that Jesus is the Son of God.

We live between these First and Second Comings of Christ. More than two thousand years ago Jesus was born of a virgin. That was His First Coming. We now await His Second Coming when the rest of Isaiah's prophecy will be fulfilled. In His Second Coming, Christ will come to reign.

Isaiah looked beyond the birth of Jesus and predicted His Second Coming and His millennial reign. When Jesus comes again, the government will be upon His shoulder, and He will reign in righteousness.

As we again approach the day we observe as His birthday, we should honor Him, worship Him, and praise Him.

December 25

The First Christmas in Heaven

The poem below was written by a 14 year old boy who was dying with a brain tumor. He died on December 14, 1997.

"I see the countless Christmas trees around the world below,
With tiny lights like Heaven's stars reflecting in the snow.
The sight is so spectacular, please wipe away the tear.
For I am spending Christmas with Jesus Christ this year.
"I hear the many Christmas songs that people hold so dear,
But the sound of music can't compare with the choir up here.
I have no words to tell you the joy their voices bring,
For it is beyond description to hear the angels sing.
"I know how much you miss me. I see the pain inside your heart.

But I am not so far away; We really aren't apart.
So be happy for me, dear ones. You know I hold you
     dear,
And be glad I'm spending Christmas with Jesus
Christ this year.
"I send you each a special gift from my heavenly
home above.
I send you each a memory of my undying love.
Love is a gift more precious than pure gold.
It was always most important in the stories Jesus told.
"Please love and keep each other as my father used
     to do,
For I can't count the blessings or love he has for each
     of you.
So have a merry Christmas, and wipe away that tear.
Remember, I am spending Christmas with Jesus
Christ this year."

December 26

Praise Ye the Lord

*"Let my mouth be filled with thy praise and with
thy honour all the day"* (Psa. 71:8).

The word "praise" is used 132 times in the book
of Psalms alone. That tells us how important it is to
praise God. In Psalm 147:1 we read, *". . . it is good
to sing praises unto our God . . ."*

The Heritage Dictionary gives the following definitions of praise: *The expression of commendation,
or admiration. The extolling or exaltation of a deity.
A reason for praise; merit. To express warm appro-
bation. To extol, exalt or worship.* Our Saviour is worthy of all these and more.

Our God is high and holy. He is worthy of all our
praise. We will praise Him for ever in Heaven, so we
should get in practice in this life.

Praising God fills the heart with gladness and joy, and it will make the day go better. We should start every day with praise to our God. We can praise Him in worship, in prayer, in song, and in service.

December 27

Draw Near to God

"Draw nigh to God, and he will draw nigh to you . . ." (James 4:8).

"But is good for me to draw near to God . . ." (Psa. 73:28).

We need to draw near to God every day. We need Him in every trial we face, and we need Him in every decision we have to make. The way to have God near us is for us to draw near to Him.

In order to draw near to God, we must confess and forsake every sin. It is our part to confess our sins; it is God's part to forgive our sins and to cleanse us from all unrighteousness, (1 John 1:9).

We should start every day with prayer. We should come into God's presence with praise and worship. We should commit our way to Him and seek His guidance for the day. We should seek God's will in all that we do. That will bring us to the place of perfect peace. That peace can go with us through the day, and when the day has ended and we can go to bed and sleep in perfect peace.

The day may bring vexations and trials. When it does, it is well to pause, to whisper a prayer, and to remember that God is a present help. There may be hard choices to make. When there are, we must remember that God is near to guide us. We can lean upon Him instead of trying to make our own decisions. Indeed it is good to draw near to God.

December 28
Seeking the Old Paths

"Thus saith the LORD, Stand ye in the ways, and see, and ask for the old paths, where is the good way, and walk therein, and ye shall find rest for your souls . . ." (Jer. 6:16).

Paths lead somewhere. The wrong path leads to the wrong destination. The right path leads to the right destination. The path of God's leading is always the right path. We should find it and walk in it.

The path we follow was made by feet that walked that way before. Our footsteps will also leave a trail for others to follow. That is another reason for following the old paths.

Footsteps leave a lasting trail. Many years ago herds of buffalo made trails as they migrated, and Buffalo Trace, as they are called, are still visible today. There is no way to know how long the path we make will last and how many generations will follow it. It is most important that our footsteps lead in the right direction.

New paths are not necessarily better paths. They never are in spiritual matters. God's paths are perfect. Man is imperfect, and the ways he charts are also imperfect. Walking in the path of God's choosing will bring perfect peace, and we will find rest for our souls.

December 29
How to Find God

"Oh that I knew where I might find him! . . ." (Job 23:3).

". . . thou shalt find him, if thou seek him with all thy heart and with all thy soul" (Deut. 4:29).

In Job's darkest hour, with property gone, children

gone, health gone, the support of his wife gone, with not a friend to encourage him, and with not a star of hope shining upon his pathway, he cried, *"Oh that I knew where I might find him . . . "* In our darkest hours we are also likely to question how we can find God.

We are promised that we will find God when we seek Him earnestly. It is well to remember that God is always near. He knows when we have problems. He knows when we are hurting, and His Holy Spirit is with us to comfort us. We only need to believe in Him, and to cast our care upon Him.

December 30
Marching by Faith

"Behold the ark of the covenant of the Lord of all the earth passeth over before you into Jordan" (Josh. 3:11).

Israel had wandered in the wilderness for forty years. Now they were ready to cross the Jordan into the land God had promised to give them, but the river was overflowing its banks. God had planned it that way, for He wanted to prove to the people that He was the God of miracles and that He was with them. Trials often come to us today for just the same reason.

Reason told Israel to wait until the river ran down, but faith told them to cross in God's time. God had promised to go before them. Their crossing would glorify Him and strengthen their faith.

What a scene it must have been as the priest, with the people following, marched toward the swollen river carrying the ark of God. The river told them that they could not cross now, but God had told them that He would go before them. They believed God and kept marching. We also sometimes have to march when it seems that there is no way to go forward.

God honored their faith, and when the feet of the priests touched the water, an invisible dam stopped the river from flowing. The water backed up behind the dam, and the water below it flowed down the valley. The river bed was soon empty, and the people were able to cross. Their faith triumphed, and they were soon in the promised land. Our faith can open the way before us also, and we can cross impossible rivers.

December 31

The Blessing of Contentment

"But godliness with contentment is great gain" *(1 Tim. 6:6).*

"And having food and raiment let us be therewith content" (1 Tim. 6:8).

Years ago in grade school I learned a salient truth. It was stated as a kind of accepted law. It read as follows: "There is no end of human wants and desires." I have never forgotten that statement, and my observations and experience have demonstrated its truth. Most people are never satisfied, no matter what they possess. For that reason they are never content.

It is possible to be content with only food, water, clothes, and shelter, but most of us have never learned that lesson. Being right with God and being satisfied with what we have can bring contentment, and that indeed is great gain.

We have more material possessions in this day than people in the past ever dreamed of having, yet many are not satisfied. Kings of other days would have given half of their kingdoms for an automobile or a television, but it is doubtful if they would have been long satisfied if they had possessed them. Things do not satisfy. Being right with God brings real peace of mind and heart.

Books by Dr. Louis Arnold

Dr. Arnold is a greatly beloved author. Thousands praise his books, and hundreds order each new book before it is off the press. People love both his novels and his Bible study books.

Great Inspirational Fiction

Readers appreciate the strong characters Dr. Arnold creates, his powers of description, and his gripping, emotion-filled stories.

Legend of Old Faithful, hardcover $19.99

Out of the Night, hardcover $19.99

Fathoms Deep, hardcover $19.99

Riverman, softcover . . . . $ 9.99

Riverman (Audio) read by author $12.99

Sunshine Valley, softcover . . . . $ 9.99

Euroclydon, softcover . . . . $ 9.99

Lucinda of Perryville, softcover . . . . $ 9.99

A Girl Named Candy, softcover . . . . $ 9.99

The Angel of Dragonpoint, softcover. . . . . . . $ 9.99

Birdman, softcover . . . . $ 9.99

Other Arnold Books

When Will the Tribulation Begin? scover . . . $ 9.99

Spiritual Realities, softcover . . . . $ 9.99

Day Starters (best-selling devotional) scover . . . . $ 9.99

Family and Friends Cookbook (J. Arnold) . . . . . . $ 9.99

Great Preachers I Have Known, scover . . . . $ 9.99

Key to Understanding the Revelation, sc . . . $11.99

Day Starters #2, softcover $11.99

Revivals are Possible, softcover . . . . $ 9.99

Arnold Publications --2440 Bethel Road -- Nicholasville, KY 40356 Phone 1-800-854-8571